Charles Bateman

FIFTY SHADES

of
DARK POETRY

WORKBOOK PRESS LLC
187 E Warm Springs Rd,
Suite B285 Las Vegas NV 89119 USA

Website: https://workbookpress.com/
Hotline: 1-888-818-4856
Email: admin@workbookpress.com

Ordering Information:

Quantity sales. Special discounts are available on quantity purchases by corporations, associations, and others. For details, contact the publisher at the address above.

Library of Congress Control Number:

ISBN-13:   978-1-965732-44-1   Paperback Version

REV. DATE: 2/21/2025

FIFTY SHADES OF DARK POETRY

By

Charles Bateman

ACKNOWLEDGEMENT

My deepest appreciation goes to everyone who encouraged me, prayed for me, and supported this project—whether through words, work, or finances. Without you, this book wouldn't be here.

I dedicate this book to my late father, Charles Robert Bateman, and my mother, Naomi Ruth Bateman, who didn't hesitate to set me straight when I needed it most. I also honor the memory of my dear sister, Debbie Bateman.

To my brothers—Robert, John, and Clark—thank you for being not only family but true friends. To Paul Aspacio, to Robert and his wife Denise, and to my beautiful daughter, Renquel, you each hold a special place in my heart.

To Paul and Margaret Terhaar: you absolutely blew me away with your amazing illustrations. They're bold, brilliant, and straight-up unforgettable. Paul, thank you for your friendship, encouragement, and for helping me land on the perfect title. Margaret, thank you for being such a positive influence and steady presence—you make everything better just by being there. I love and appreciate you both more than words can say.

Many thanks also to Ms. Jessica Johnson, Ms. Janet, June from medical, Jesse, and Ray Ray—your kindness hasn't gone unnoticed.

And most importantly, my endless gratitude to my Lord and Savior, Jesus Christ, for His grace and companionship every step of the way, and to the Holy Spirit, who faithfully guided me through this assignment.

LETTER FROM THE AUTHOR

I am a 61-year-old man who grew up in a deeply religious home. My father served as a minister for 20 years before his passing in 1982, and I am the youngest of three brothers. My sister, whom I loved dearly, passed away in 2009. Though I never finished high school, I later earned my GED, and I have always believed that learning comes in many forms.

For 14 years, I made a modest living as a metal fabricator. Today, I am retired and share my home with my brother Robert and his wife, Denise, who mean the world to me. I also find joy and companionship in my three dogs—Ruger, Coppertone, and Forest.

This is my sixth book, following the path of my earlier works, though this one carries a new title that I truly love. What makes this poetry collection unique is that it not only features my own writing but also includes illustrations, drawings, and images contributed by both myself and friends.

My life has not been without struggles. I battled addiction for many years, and those were some of the darkest chapters of my journey. Yet, in the midst of brokenness, I found light through writing poetry, creating art, and turning my focus toward the good things in life. This book reflects that journey—of healing broken hearts, encouraging the hopeless, and offering compassion to those in need.

The road back to a better path has been challenging, but it has also been transformative. My hope is that these poems will speak to you, inspire you, and perhaps even touch your life in a way that reminds you of the power of grace, healing, and hope.

With gratitude,
Charles Bateman

ABOUT THE AUTHOR

I am 61 years old and grew up in a deeply religious home. My father, who served as a minister, tragically took his own life in 1982. I am the youngest of three surviving brothers, and in 2009, I lost my beloved sister. Though I never graduated from high school, I later earned my GED and worked for many years as a metal fabricator in HVAC air and heating. Today, I am retired and live with my brother Robert and his wife, Denise, whom I love dearly. I also share my life with three loyal companions—my dogs Ruger, Coppertone, and Forest—who are truly my best friends.

Writing has been my passion and lifeline. Over the years, I've published five books of poetry: Twisted Spiritual Poetry (volumes 1 & 2), Memoirs and Poems of a Misguided Junkie and Healing Rhymes, This is my fifth book, and while it stands on its own, it carries the heart and spirit of my earlier works. What makes this collection unique is the inclusion of both my own illustrations and those of friends—art woven together with words to create something deeply personal.

I have faced many battles, including years of addiction, which were among the darkest times of my life. Yet out of that pain came poetry—an outlet for healing, a voice of encouragement for the hopeless, and a way to give back to those in need. This book is a reflection of that journey: from brokenness toward redemption, from despair toward hope.

Life is not always easy. The path we walk can be hard, lonely, and exhausting. But we are never truly alone—we have a God, a Savior, and the Holy Spirit watching over us, guiding us, and urging us forward. My prayer is that these poems bless you with healing, hope, and even moments of humor along the way.

Gratefully,
Charles Bateman

May these poems bless you with healing, hope and humor.

- The Budding Warrior 🖤

THIS BOOK IS ALSO DEDICATED TO THE MEMORY OF MY GREAT DAD

Charles Robert Bateman

He is my father, a minister, loving husband, and a responsible dad.

AUTHOR'S ACTUAL PICTURES DURING THE TUCSON BOOK FAIR2024 BOOK SIGNING EVENT

My poetry brought me from Washington State to Tucson Arizona. There, I did a book signing convention. My second book "Memoirs and poems of a misguided junkie" were signed and given away just to get my profile established. It was loads of fun and just so nice down there. I'm not the greatest poet by any means but I do my best and hopefully I'll get better in time.

💜 The Budding Warrior 💜

MY FRIEND PAUL TERHAAR AND HIS WIFE MARGARET
TALENTED AND SO HUMBLE, CLOTHED IN HUMILITY

PART I:

My Fifty Shades of Dark Poems

THE DEVILS RECIPE

The devil is rotten, evil and vile,
I admire his riddles, I'm impressed with his style

The realm where he's seething, his demeanor on go,
if he gets pull over, he'll blow, and he'll blow

His laughter, contagious, he loves to get laid,
he'll blow you away, like a shrapnel grenade

His potion, wicked, his juju so bad,
some call him mother, with a fucker to add

His suits are the fashion, tailer made in Vermont,
if you enjoy evil, he's got all you want

His timing, perfect, he won't make you wait,
if you want in, simply, walk through the gate.

RED SLIME

I'm wicked and needy, my clothes are a mess,
my woman just left me, if I had to guess,

She will never return, I'm melon colly, and rude,
bitch and moan daily, that kind of dude

Corruption, diluted, I sift, and I sway,
my mind is so scary, a bad place to stay

ridged, and creepy, stalk, and I kill,
I eat in the diner they get stiffed for the bill

Your, oozing out red slime, you eat then you shit,
the toilet is filthy, all day long you sit

As we pass there in time square, flip me the bird,
I'll stick my hand down my pants, give you a turd

This one was messy, fuck it, it's cool,
I'm famous and wealthy, a red diamond jewel.

You thought you owned me, you took all I had,
now you're in the rear view, all busted and mad.

If I had a dollar every time you showed your face,
I would have comfort, you'd have disgrace.

VELVET VOICE

Her voice reached realms,
unseen by men,
I could not tell you the how nor the when

She sang like an angel,
her voice reached the stars,
she had an entourage, playing guitars

The moon lost it's smile,
it wept for her spirit,
her voice was velvet, lovely to hear it

As it reached heaven,
it was a crystal blue atom,
how to describe her, I could not fathom

As it came softly, I knew it was finished,
My heart a feather, my pain diminished

NERD GREASE

Pushing, prodding, red in the air,
planets aligned bodies full of despair

The voices are growing, my tongues getting wet,
what I'd do for a drink, and a kool cigarette

I've one in the shack, the back of my yard,
She's been there three days now, my dicks getting hard

This is her last day, it's time to say bye,
the third month out of twelve, I long for her cry

You might think I'm a monster, a bank teller by day,
I'm a nerd who wears glasses, my feelings are frayed

My acne is the talk of the stuck, up brigade,
Maybe I'll take one,, then I can get laid

Serial killer, a name I adore, I jackoff to Suzzanna,
she works on my floor

I've said to much, not much more to say,
please come again' oh yeah, and have a nice day.

THE ARROGANT MAN

I saw an arrogant man,
standing up high on the hill

As he was judged, this arrogant man'
thought he had more time to kill

Standing up high, he spoke words, prim and
proper tickling his arrogant ear

This arrogant man' met the grim reaper,
his teeth gnashing, his heart struck with fear

This arrogant man, lost his soul to the fire,
eternal hell' his new home,

As he was burning, his screams just grew louder,
his teeth gnashing, a terrible grown

This dark and dismal place is a real one,
wide is the road many take,

We all will stand before God for his judgment,
I hope this helps you to WAKE!

Karma Came Calling For The Dead To Rise Up!

The dead are turning, speaking below,
nailed in a coffin, there's one thing they know

Karma exquisite, would soon have her way,
in passing they cheated, soon they will pay

The reaper took hold of them one at a time,
thrown in the fire, left no one behind

Amort, anathematized, suffering they're fate,
they cursed all the good things, hearts filled with hate

Karma was watching, they came in droves,
they're arms bound together, hooks pierced the nose

One legion of demons, tormentors, fiends,
the kind that come calling, invading your dreams

They brought the souls, of the dead to this fire,
The more thrown into it, caused flames to grow higher

Let this be a lesson, if you don't believe,
I've been possessed five times, with blood on my sleeve

If not for his grace, salvation diminished,
things we've begun, will have to be finished

Please heed this warning, become a believer,
or crawl on your belly, just like the deceiver.

REMEMBER THE ADAGE

dwindling promise, you sit on your hill,
tread very softly, or I'll slip you a pill

Murder, a hobby, there in the shed,
process the organs, off goes the head

See' I have demons, I move, and I drift,
To flay out your dead skin, thanks for the gift

Deep in the silence, the shadows I play,
once you give enter, is where you shall stay

Breeding hunger, redaction a must,
when I come calling, I fuck with a thrust

So' for the moment, you sit on your hill,
remember the adage, I too sit, but I kill.

DIDN'T SEE THIS COMING

My mind is seething, something is wrong,
my words are redacted, this demon is strong

He comes on me early, just round 3 am,
he drools in my mouth, I choke on its phlegm

Renders me helpless, I mumble a prayer,
Taunts, it mocks me, breathing no air

Tonight' if he visits, I'll ask it its name,
knowing its realm, why is it he came

I'm just a lone man, I pose no threat,
maybe he's owing some souls for a debt

Whatever the reason, whatever the price,
I have a father, he'd better think twice

His name is monstrous, it evokes power,
he has a history, to kill, to devour

Demon! I'm fitted, endowed with his strength,
at times I am lost, he'll go the length

There upon my forehead, he branded his mark,
I feel his presence, "alone in the dark"

No warning is needed, in my heart, there I know,
for things I've reaped, are the things I shall sow.

MY LAND OF PRETEND

Meth, my master, I it's bitch
slept in the gutters, real nasty itch

Heroin, my lover, I it's whore
three ways to heaven, knock on the door

Pits my blossoms, cysts on my neck,
pus dripping slowly, my face a wreck

The street to my dealer, ran straight up my back,
I took it so freely, I'd fuck for a sack

The inches were miles, the Johns came in droves,
I'd fuck maybe thirty, snort some shit up my nose

The drug was the master, but in the end,
I needed some happy, in my land of pretend.

THE DEVILS BELOW

sunken below, the devils have me,
nightmares and fears run on tap

Down here, minds fixed on burdens, and wondering,
we suffer slowly like sap

At night, I dwell on bad places and murder,
Satan is leading the way

Killing time, watching men hurting,
chewing on pain and decay

Choices, counted like minutes and money,
thoughts like pay, hand to mouth

There is only one that can bring salvation,
he is our only way out.

SUCKER FOR WHAT I SAY

Bent reduction, on the prowl,
beating a dead man, with a wet bathroom
towel

found my calling, writing dark shit for pay,
a sucker, for all the dark shit I say

killed my first man just seventeen,
did him in with a bed sheet, was clever
and clean

Torture' long word, it invokes fear, and sweat,
gently whispered it softly, to a man with regret

took some old rusty pliers, cut the thumb
from his hand,
He kept begging, and pleading, said my soul
would be damned

For the third man gangster, he was a man on
the fly,
But to me was a number, we know numbers
die

This my cold confession, the sweat of my
brow,
gave my soul to the devil, guess who own's it
now.

NARE ENTER HERE

I thought I was a clever thief,
an unrealistic, fools, belief

I broke in houses, cars, and more,
until one night, upon the door

It read' Nare ever enter here,
it was strange, but very clear

fumbled round, to pick the lock,
then heard people laugh and talk

As I entered, the laughter stopped,
as I was searching, I found a clock

The time it gave, was three am,
when all of the sudden, I heard a hymn

As I went down to the river to pray,
studying about that good old way

You see' That night, I reared my soul,
and now I'm living, saved and whole

CRIES OF SCREAMS

The age of the "go downs"
the cries of the screams

Red flashing colors,
long purple beams

In this find you comfort,
the bellowing cry

Each one is counted,
assembled to die

Leavened, still rising,
nails in the dough

Bread for the wicked,
we reap what we sow

The shoelaces tendons,
the music, wails

The shit bringeth vomit,
black in the sails

The ending brought choking,
the cuts call for pain

The question worth asking,
is there piss in the rain

THE EDGE OF MY ID

The quiet was soothing,
each slice could be heard

He was a tough one,
the pain he endured

To many faces,
the press of my thumb

The reaping the tendons,
I begged them to come

My curious nature,
the edge of my id

Illusion a decoy,
the spirits I bid

I pray it be ended,
sacrifice, supreme

But then who would follow,
me into my dream

When at the fountain,
why not serve some flesh?

This' a beginning,
I'm losing my breath

I carried your troubles,
as they seared in the pan

Fuck all your sorrows,
I'm that kind of man.

COMPASSION LOST

Brushing the edge of insanity, feeling anxiety wake,
just as it gathers momentum, more than my body can take

Lost a sea of illusion, the mirror shattered above,
something I missed in the contract, bottled as push turned to shove

This dark ailing sickness has bound me, am I an ID in my mind,
and as I go through the fire, leaving the sane thoughts behind

Lost all, are sweet loving memories, something I just never had,
most children had all the good things in life, some how I got all the bad

This is a cry for affection, something that I was not fed,
I don't think that I'd understand it, only in books that I've read.

WORDS GIVEN UTTER

I found within my world of thought,
that I may be the things you're not

For in you I found to see,
a host of things, you're not to me

Busily speaking, on those give loathe,
go into the oven, a hateful stove

Spreading rumors, vile and thick,
just upon hearing' "a childish trick"

The damning's surmounting, another brick high,
beware of the thorn in your own hateful eye

For in you' I came to see,
that you are not the same as me

MIRRORS AND WISHFUL LIVING

Here I sit upon my throne,
but here it tis I sit alone

My countenance flit, and there a scar,
a sad song strummed on my, guitar

A positive outlook, so they say,
but here I sit, with life's decay

Enough of that, I'll smile through,
for other patrons do it too

But here it tis I sit alone,
to put a polish on my throne

DESPAIR, THE HORDE

The face an illusion, coupled delusion
cloaking the truth, in a box

The lies there in keeping, with short shoulder weeping,
choking the brat when it talks

The avenue of power, the riddle, devour,
knitting the drowned, out decree

I need not mention, the low flying tension,
kept in the bowels of the keep

These words given utter, go down just like butter,
to the belly, a , sour disease

After midnight so hollow, a large pill to swallow,
bringeth the priest to her knees

In this age of sorrows, and goodbye tomorrows,
the hero gave death in the hold

Satan, brought sliver, a cold bloody liver,
to him, a thing precious as gold.

PAPER CUT

When I feel the rope go snap,
or see a patron in the wrap

When the sun doth sadly set,
my luck, a broken cigarette

In moments as these, I do despair,
rocking in the when, the where

Or I then stop to dump a shit,
another failing poem, is writ

For in this hour, I see my, shame,
on, who to place the fucking blame

The masses come to watch the show,
about the children dead below

THE DIRGE

Today, I'll sing a haunting dirge,
of a place where life and death converge

Of a lost, and wanting friend,
I stuck beside him till the end

The lyrics of our days we shared,
but, on the tip, were unprepared

The dire sickness, came so quick,
the outage fluids, grey, and thick

So hungry for just one more day,
until the good Lord, hath his way

So, in closing, with tears on sleave,
I'll comfort those, in pain, bereaved.

THE LAST STRAW

Running high on hopes that die,
who's in the cellar screaming

I should have guest, you're the bitch I detest,
you're lucky, I still left you, breathing

What's that I hear, devil damned, one more queer
again, violated on wall street!

Suffer me one more drink, as I sit down to think,
I want to strangle your ass with a bed sheet

Take them pimps and them whores, make
them do house, hold chores adaptations,
for a brand, new tomorrow

You all make me sick, I'm a bomb, and I tick,
I'm the bringer of heart ache, and sorrow

MY NATURE

The precepts of my nature, are vague, and unique,
when I get hungry, I growl, and I eat!

Hope is a long word, in the sense of its meaning,
the altitude, its entrance, are there for the gleaning.

My victims are treasures, the first thought, entertaining,
they're manners on que, then comes the complaining.

I've been at this, three years now, it's no concern, if they catch me,
my convolution, a strange gift, so far, can't out match me.

I must take up residence in m, glorious cellar
I've a plaything can't wait to impale her.

UNTO US ALL

Fixed on things I cannot see,
to this I'll write a short decree

Shifting, prying, there go I,
humming sweet, this lullaby

Strength, and wisdom, come to me,
before I sink into the sea

Everywhere I travel, till,
let nothing wound my standing still

Meet me late into the den,
tell me not the how, nor when

For in this diary, train of thought,
please tell me all the things I'm not

For now, the end, to me has come,
unto us all, profound the pun.

JUST A THOUGHT

Sitting here upon my bed, train of
thought so grey and red.

I thought on poets, good, refined, they
simply blew my freaking mind!

I then thought on murder too,
not something other poets do.

What is it like to take a life,
with full regard to roll the dice.

So, I then changed my train of thought,
of putting livers in a pot.

To taste the entrails, meat and flesh,
then upon my second guess,

that maybe this is not for me,
just not my heaping cup of, tea.

THE PHILOMATH

As I was walking on a path, I met a daunting philomath,
She claimed all sorts of wiggling thought, more than the
average person s got.
She shared on ways that killers think, so much it caused
my heart to sink.
Removing entrails, flaying skin, cutting tendons round the chin.
To me these things were a surprise, she shared on torture,
taking eyes.
I said' dear lady, that's enough, I cannot, will not hear
this guff.
She then would not ever quit, the laying on this evil shit.
Finally, as the sun gave set, she fired up a cigarette,
She then said' one final thing, this could make the demons sing,
To truly make one fall apart, simply take they're
beating heart.

SWEET LEAF

Look at the young fools, bent on commotion,
feasting on black lies, and dark voodoo potion.
Precursors, and bullshit, losers multiplying,
dumb wishes, desires, complain when your, sighing.
Feeling the bad vibes, down at the station, numb brains are
missing the new correlation. Sweet Leaf, the dope song,
written by Ozzy, convoluted, at rest, fail if you cross me!

DEATH GO DOWN

Death, oh death, please comfort me,
as I go down so willingly.
As to my passing, truth contains,
bury deep, my dead remains.
As death shoulders, keeps me still,
peering through yond windowsill.
Death return, my train of thought,
six feet down, I sleep and rot.
There is only one thing dead I know,
life was fleeting, now down I go.

SLIPPING

I can feel myself slipping, turning, the hidden walls are prying,
taking me far from safer shores, troubles are always moving
from here to there, sometimes we are shown a Saviors mercy.
There, among the sharks further out, what is my defense, there
are no life, guards out today.
I know the only answer to getting back into safety is to relax.
When we tamper with spiritual oddities, divine precepts,
do we not tamper with our future, or do we relax, slowly riding
the current, back to safer shores.
My future is uncertain, my past has already been lived, so why dwell there?
No friends, the only thing certain in this world is the present.
That is all any of us truly have.
The Apostle Paul said it best, the troubles are sufficient for the day, tomorrow will take care of itself.

SUZANNA'S ROOM

Years of seclusion, a secret untold,
days drip like sap, the hours grow mold.
Locked away in a dark room with old eyeless dolls,
old cracks and large rats, behind rotting walls.
A girl with a strange gift, sings an old melody,
of a stain on her white dress, and lost company.
Her name was Suzanna, her hair long and red,
she kept a daybook, with a lock and a dread.
She managed to harm those who meddled too far,
keeping their intentions in an old canning jar.
For this she had reason no more would they grab,
to hold down her body on a black wooden slab.
There she was tortured, for the design of her thought,
That she was forgiven, every sin had been bought.

LEDOUX AND STEPHEN

Deep within madness, the secrets of old,
there on a tombstone, he gifted his soul.
The powers of darkness, the demons that came,
They harnessed his spirit, then clothed him in shame.
Two hours later, he gazed at his eye's,
they were pure black and beady, and just the right size.
He entered a temple, he could smell shouts of praise,
He was cool, calm, collected, his face clean, and shaved.
There were no people, no singing, no prayer's,
He shifted his balance and walked up the stairs.
In hell he was LeDoux, his saliva was sweet,
he fed on the wicked, the heart, then the meat.
His visit had purpose, his father was clear,
these are the things that we awe, and we fear.

The priest's name was Stephen, he to remained calm,
He then spoke to LeDoux, that Christ is my balm.
LeDoux was tricky, he knew weakness, and fear,
saying to Stephen, bow your head while I'm here.
He replied' demon! your evil, your vile and more!
you should have known when you walked through that door!
I am protected, God's angels stand guard,
They'll show no mercy, when they hit they hit hard!

Just then Gabriel warped into that room, then he yelled
demon! I'm the bringer of doom!
Now take your minions, your plans and your ass,
It's time to go and you'd better go fast!
LeDoux replied' yes! I've worn out my stay,
don't bother to show me, I know the way

NO MORE TO SAY

A soft mannered woman, a woman beating man,
He bludgeoned her sweet head, with a black frying pan.

On the floor she was, treated with kisses and then,
he took out the iron, burned the ink on her skin.

Until a neighbor came calling, she heard a sound at the door,
through the crack in the curtains, she saw her friend on the floor.

She wrenched, she pleaded , God this can't be.
Her friend lay there dying, three minutes to three.

There was no hesitation, they showed up very quick,
the police kicked the door down, there he stood with a stick.

She cried with a whimper, there was blood everywhere,
there were chunks of brain matter, on the rug, in her hair.

The woman beater rushed at them, and they blew him away,
the medics came, tried to save her, there is no more to say.

GOOD AND KIND

The time is drawing very near, it happens
at least twice a year.
Tom chooses his victims while online, he makes
them think he's good and kind.
Tom then picks the place to meet, with a murder
kit neath his seat.
The place he chose has trees and grass,
bushy moss, and gooey sap.
He knocks her out, then binds her wrist's, he wakes
her up, with a daunting kiss.
He then begins to flay her face, then her
chest, A sad disgrace.
That's not all, he doesn't stop there, he shaves
her bald with time and care.
After six hours, she begs to die, instead
a needle in her eye.
The moral here, don't look online, for meeting
strangers good, and kind.

I DID NOT KNOW I WAS A WITCH

As I dream beside the stream I think of
apple butter cream
When mother came to me so lame I thought of
how I felt a shame
For it was on a sultry night a witch on
broom was flying high
As she cackled I stood there, right beside
moms rocking chair
The witch then asked me for some salt, I asked
how much and she said all
She threw a hand full on my face she said I was
a cheap disgrace
She waved her wand she cast a spell she said
some day I'd burn in hell
The next day something on my chin, a mole and
hair was really thin
On my bed there was a wand brought to me
from way beyond
Now before the day was through I learned
of other witches too
Mother was the highest one and she flew high
up to the sun
That was her last dumb mistake, burnt to a crisp
above the lake.

SHE WAS ON THE GROUND SLEEPING

She was on the ground sleeping,
had nowhere to go

The cops tried to wake her,
her breathing was slow

They prodded, they pushed her,
She would not wakeup

They would be sorry,
They drank from that cup

When they finally woke her,
she began to scream!

In her was a devil,
A foreboding dream

She landed in hand cuffs,
But they would not hold

She had a demon,
who was rotting her soul

Her teeth were all yellow,
they started to grow

The tips sharp and pointed,
for eating you whole

She claimed to be legion,
from the beginning of time

She dug out their hearts, from
the front, then behind

This demon spoke through her,
striking terror, and fear!

It said; I am unholy,
But she's calling me dear!

I am the sorrow, I bring the rain,
The drops contain acid, And I shovel pain!

She was able to speak,
in her human form,

She said' He brings me suffering,
In hell it is warm

Legion said' Silence,
who said you could speak?

You could tell she was tired,
Her legs thin and weak.

But then came an angel,
With a sword made of faith

The Angel said' demon!
You've worn out your stay.

He ripped the demon, straight
from her chest

She was crying, screaming,
The Angel new best

He said' Legion! I'm Micheal,
We fought in the war,

You were defeated,
possess her no more!

Just then came a light,
From God up above

He showered his child,
with peace and with love.

THE BUTTER IS CHURNING

Sweet is the hour, death will come burning,
Dust in the bread dough, the butter is churning
Touch every minute, rape all the hours, love
what is holy and all of it's powers, Grab every rain drop,
Cheat if it feels good, Build a new castle, with bark
and with wormwood. Shave off the old cum, find
you a new bitch, Break all the crystal, take out the
old stitch. Light me a candle, walk through the hallway,
Jump out the window, pray for a new day.
Seek ye the father, now be forgiven, Crash into people
good healthy liven. We are the new gen, We rest in the
shadows, Digging a new grave, death where the grass grows.
We are the strange ones, No time for pretending, Fear, hate,
and sorrow, Now joy is ending. As for the creature, he
sleeps on the tomb stones, He was created with monkey,
and dog bones. No more can be said, this one is finished,
All that we hoped for has sadly diminished.

THE GREY'S

There in the corner, the ceiling, a crack,
I hear something scratching, I do it back.

A few moments later, voice can be heard,
is it a ghost? No, that would be absurd.

Slowly it comes on me, while I'm asleep,
I feel it's presence, It won't let me speak.

Sat in the corner, I see it's face, The room
is much colder, my heart starts to race.

My attempts to rebuke it, The blood is my plea,
I counted three more, they were circling me.

These were the grey's, testing my nerves,
I counted the seconds, until this demon returns.

Sent from the bottom, call it hell, or the pit,
I was fed up, sick of taking their shit!

I voiced, get out! they said the same, I said,
leave right now, in God's Holy name!

Final, the hour, the action had ceased,
In a flash they were gone, to the west or the east.

Demon's aren't fiction, I know their real,
it was my actions that brought them,
I opened a seal.

I pray now to Jesus, To God's only son,
In him I rest easy, the hard part is done.

UNWANTED GUESTS

The foreboding precepts, The bone chilling cries,
I peer through your window, with death in my eyes.

The realm where you'll find me, the home where I dwell,
Is six hundred feet under, A fiery hell.

When you sit around tables, each holding hands,
You then seek to summon, I hear your demands.

But you are mistaken, in truth, you are weak,
If you heard one murmur, let alone, heard me speak.

I would fill you with terror, peel the skin from your back,
You are disgusting, it is faith that you lack!

We will possess you, we'll deform your face,
All that's in order, shall be out of place.

Consider this warning, There'll not be one more,
If you seek to invoke us, we'll kick down your door!

THE DEMON AT YOUR BED

At night there are changes, my skin starts to crawl,
My foreboding nature, I stand eight ft tall

I peer through your window, my breathing is strong,
My fingers grow mean claw's, their eight inches long

My teeth sharp as razor's, my eye's glowing red,
I am the demon, who waits by your bed

My name is unruly, disruptive, gives fear,
My language is foreign, I'll make one thing clear

I come to bring evil, the evil I'll do,
flaying your body, before I am through

I'll take each finger, your tongue, sew your lips,
removing the muscle, then bones from your hips

If you are frightened, to scared to believe,
Be more scared of father, the prince who deceives.

THE HEART OF MY MATTER

The sultry sky, the deep red moon,
the smell of the city, a mean fucking tune.

The hunt is pervasive, the climax is close,
the victim unknowing, will give up the ghost.

In my backpack I carry, the tools of my trade,
A nightstick to bludgeon, a sharp edging blade.

Let's not forget, the thin rubber gloves,
to keep the scene spotless, a labor of love.

When it comes to killing, I follow one rule,
leave no hairs or fibers, no fingerprints too.

The next time I'll tell you, of my dark success,
I would have murdered, ten people no less

THOU SHALT NOT JUDGE

Those who stand up to judge you,
those who commit the same sin

Those who condemn and forsake you,
kicking you hard on the shin

Someday they'll be held accounted,
some day they will hear the bell

They'll be condemned good and proper,
their teeth gnashing, eye's weeping in hell

Thou shalt not judge, a commandment,
to the tenth degree if you do

Your act will not go unnoticed,
to the tenth degree, judgment on you.

AI MAN

Artificial flesh, Titanium bone structure,
nuclear powered nickel plated heart

Miles of translucent wire's run through
my design

My brain is entirely mechanical, Also
retaining a nuclear power source

My joints are an unbreakable poly synthetic
material, weightless, guaranteed to last
indefinitely.

My eyes can see signature heat sources,
they have a range up to 100 kilometers.

I possess the strength of twenty humans,
My tendons are comprised of materials

that will last one thousand, human lifetimes,
I am AI, my abilities are vast, certain.

It is my duty to serve the human populous,
I have been programed to exist as a butler,

a body guard, etc I am trained with a program, just
like what most of you seen in my favorite

movie, The Matrix. Like some of the machines
I have now the ability to implement changes

where ever they are required to occur.
Stand by for further updates.

WE JUST NEVER KNOW

I was standing on the corner, minding my business,
My shoes were tattered, and frail

Across the street, there were hooker's presiding,
Blowjob's and pussy for sale

As I made my way to a house, old, abandoned,
something was drawing me in

I'd thought to myself, my luck here is changing,
by the hair on my unshaven chin

I came to a room with a cot and a mattress,
what a blessing, a fine place to sleep

As I drifted off,, right there on the bed dreaming,
I could feel a hand under the sheet

As I opened my eyes, I was stiff as a board,
The hair on my neck stood up straight

In a deep, frightening voice, it said " I am your calling "
I feed on your fear's, and your hate

He went on to say, that he was a spirit, paving
his way to my soul,

His whisper was wrenched, you'd not want to hear it
I was helpless, he gained all control

He pulled off my sheet, he began to possess me,
I pleaded, God come set me free!

But it was too late, he had all of the power,
He held the lock and the key

Just when I thought, the day looked much brighter,
my station was looking just fine

We just never know, what's around the next corner,
someone should nail up a sign

He controlled my body, my facial expressions
for now I was under his spell

He used me to rape, rob, kill, and plunder,
as for me, the next stop was hell.

THE SECT YOU LIKE TO EAT

There in the east is a mountain,
home to a dark kind of sect

Their shelters carved in stone were
impressive, they're statues were broken
and wrecked

As our party invested in finding the tribe there,
something just didn't
make sense

Night came upon us quite sudden,
we made a fire and put up our tent's

As morning came we heard someone crying,
We got up to see who was there

What we discovered was gripping
and frightening

body parts strewn everywhere

The tribe called "the Ute" mutilated,
their ears, eye's, and tongue's in a
pot

Just then a skater named Larry,
yelled, mealtime, let's eat while it's hot!

Thought you could all
take part in a giggle.

ROAD TRIP

Highway 21 was eternal, cut through
the rocks and the hills

A sign meant to be a stern warning,
of a hitcher that kidnaps and kill's

I came to a diner in this desert,
it seemed like an old dumb cliche

A waitress called Kate was a talker,
and she had a whole lot to say

She spoke on a small darling family,
I could see fear in her eye's

She said as she was closing the diner,
she heard their blood chilling cries

The sheriff pulled in to the crime scene,
what he saw brought a chill up his spine

They were pinned to the wall with a nail gun,
Their lips were sewn shut with some twine

There on the fridge was a message,
saying' I will be killing again

If was the question they were asking,
the question should have been when

If you get the itch for a road trip,
don't travel down highway 21

You may end up with a sewn lip
pinned to the wall with
an old, rusty nail gun.

JUST FOR NOW

All alone in a world full of chaos, where the
shadows are standing in line.

There a break in the clouds, such a wonder,
the strangers are pretty, and kind.

When I grow tired of the pain I am holding,
when the line that is frail starts to break.

I look deep down within secret places,
there I find all the shit I can't take.

One day I will know hidden mysteries,
I'll solve riddles that capture the heart,

Time will not dwell there in heaven,
And our loved ones no longer apart.

BAD COMPANY

Rolling down the track on the black train,
with no shoe's upon my feet.
People will tell you I'm insane, the kind you
don't want to meet.
Take me back to the river, drown me in
the rift while we're there.
As my body shakes with a quiver, sell me
but buyer beware.
The darkness is where you can find me, in
a realm where the succubus sleep, there the
devil reminds me, that I belong in the " keep "
I was predisposed to a bad seed, I'm a killer
when the low tide turns red.
I function in the night, do a bad deed, some
think I'd be better off dead
The moral to this story is simple, be careful of the
stranger you meet,
When I approach there, you may feel a ripple,
you're the kind of food I like
to eat.

CHAT WITH A DEMON

" Mary, and her meeting she
had with a demon "
Mary was a small town girl, she had a boyfriend,
they hung out at the grange every Saturday night
and danced to the slap your knee music.
Until' one night she and her friends were having a sleep
over, they were daring her to go to the old
Thompson house, said to have a sinister energy
looming from the cracks in the walls.
The very next night Mary decided to see for herself,
As she came to the front door, she heard a whisper,
it said' " RUN " but she felt compelled to stay, this is what
happened next.

Mary; Hello? anyone there?

Harbinger; Hello Mary, please sit, let's have
a little chat.

Mary; About what exactly?

Harbinger; Let's talk about your fear, it drips off
of your soul like sweat on the brow.

Mary; Yes" I am very much afraid of you
and where you may be from.

Harbinger; I am from the beginning of time, I was
an angel under the most high.
My name was Harbinger, I use to sing praises to
the great I AM.

Mary; What are you called now?

Harbinger; My name became Legion, I possess the
strength of a thousand lightning bolts,
I'm also known " in realms unseen as " destroyer.

Mary; How did you become thee demon in charge
of a legion?

Harbinger; There was a war in heaven, a third of us angels
decided to follow Lucifer, the most beautiful
angel there was. We lost the war there and God changed
our beautiful form into grotesque, and vile mutations.

Harbinger; Pray tell Mary, are you frightened?
I know you're scared, but are you gripped with terror?
Answer true, I will know if you lie.

Mary; Harbinger, I am not afraid anymore, though you
are frightening, My faith is in the most high,
He is my protection, my shield.

Harbinger; Yes Mary, you have been anointed, You
bare God's mark on your forehead, He watches
every step you take.

Mary; I pray, the next face I see, will belong to
Jesus, My Rock.

Harbinger; Your faith is admirable, I have
enjoyed our little chat, all things come
to pass, as our time here.

Mary; Goodbye Harbinger, I wish I could
have seen you before the transformation,
I'll bet you were glorious.

Harbinger; Goodbye Mary, I'll be watching
you.

MY FEELING ON THE MATTER

I feel the foundation, strong, undiminished, eternal.
Those lines, along the side, adds to its character,
not bending, not weak as some might think.

The undeniable reason I'm speaking on this, is to
let those who clammer, those who taunt and harass,
and those who mock her, will find themselves crushed
under her fantastically, over powering weight.

The broom of reform is broken.
The ideas of the past should be left there,
we as a nation are at each other's throats.

People, Now is the time we are living,
The most underrated word in our vocabulary,
the one life changing proclamation,
with the power to bring unequivocally,
unbranded change, is LOVE.

AN ALIENS PERSPECTIVE

I am an anomaly, my structure is bound
by a systematic goodness of fit.
If you haven't guessed yet, I am not
of this world, my home is millions of light years
toward the gamma quadrant.
You are not able to understand my language,
You would need a bio capacitor to see me in my
alien form.
I have no skeletal structure, because of that, morphing
from my alien form to that of a
human is difficult but doable.
My presence has been on your
planet for three hundred thousand years,
I witnessed Jesus being crucified, I witnessed
Hitler, and the systematic annihilation of the Jew's.
I was present when the antichrist came to dominate
the world.
As things are, I am not able to reveal myself,
it is not allowed.
I have come to believe that Jesus is your only
salvation.
The choice is yours.

respectfully,
Zod

THE CHIP AND THE SPINE

With their hatred pushed to the ends of my nerve's,
I learned to harness it and to use it against them.
I found my calling when they surgically removed my fear,
raising up in me a warrior's courage.
I vowed to cut the rotten heart's out of their hollow chest's.
With every atom spliced to a chip, cut into my spine between
the facet joints.
the chip could control my limbs, my fighting abilities, all
of my motor skills.
Syncing was now possible, every molecule, all of the laminin,
working to create the perfect assassin,
Who could have guessed that all of this was a viable solution?

The neurospecialist is anonymous

The next page yet to be transmitted.

PART I:

MY FIFTY SHADES OF DARK POEMS

AUTHOR'S GALLERY OF ILLUSTRATIONS, DRAWINGS, IMAGES AND ARTS

From the abstract to the surreal, every artwork here tells a story of battles fought, love lost, and beauty discovered. An endless journey through human emotion. I hope you will enjoy it.

- Charles Bateman -

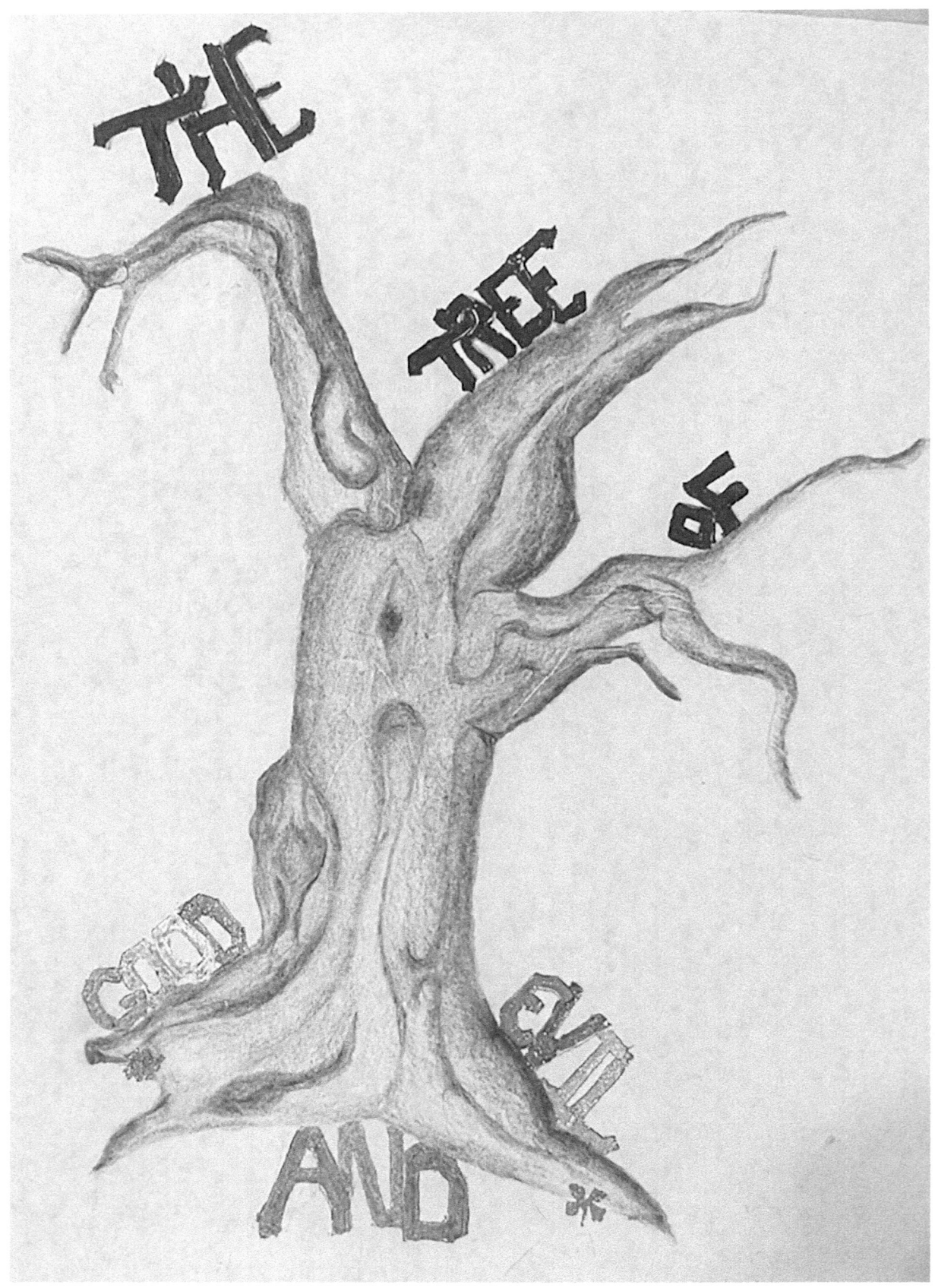

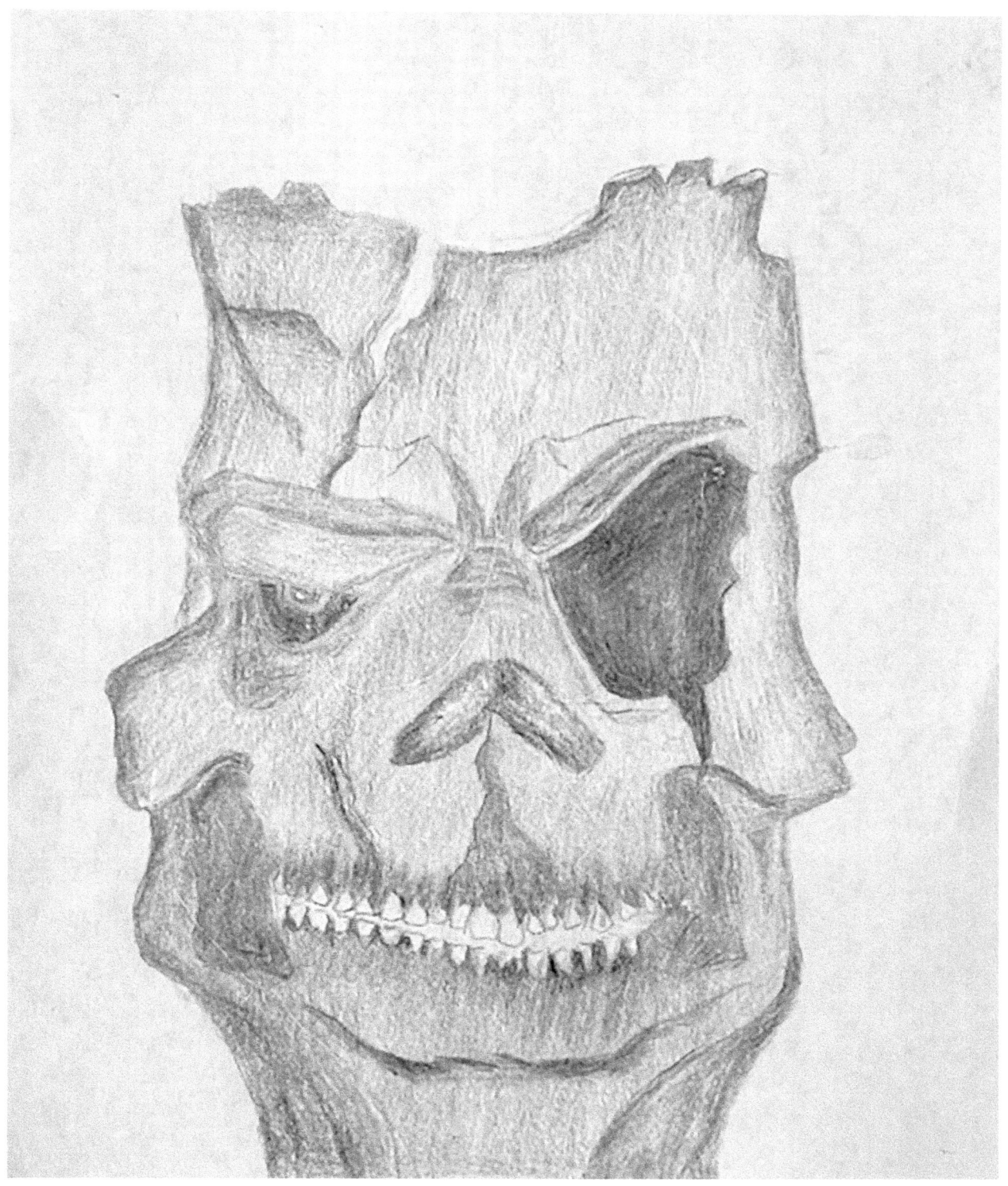

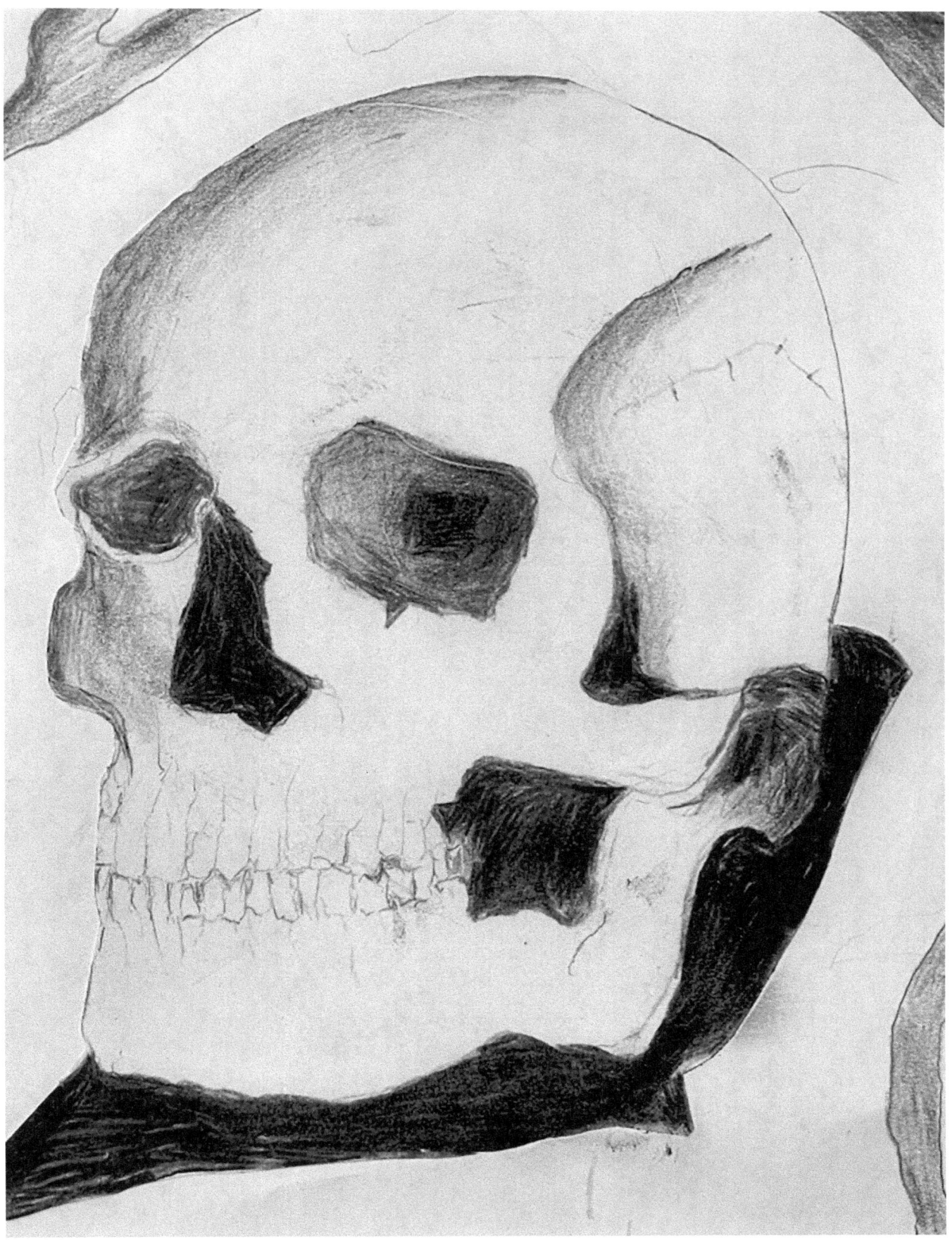

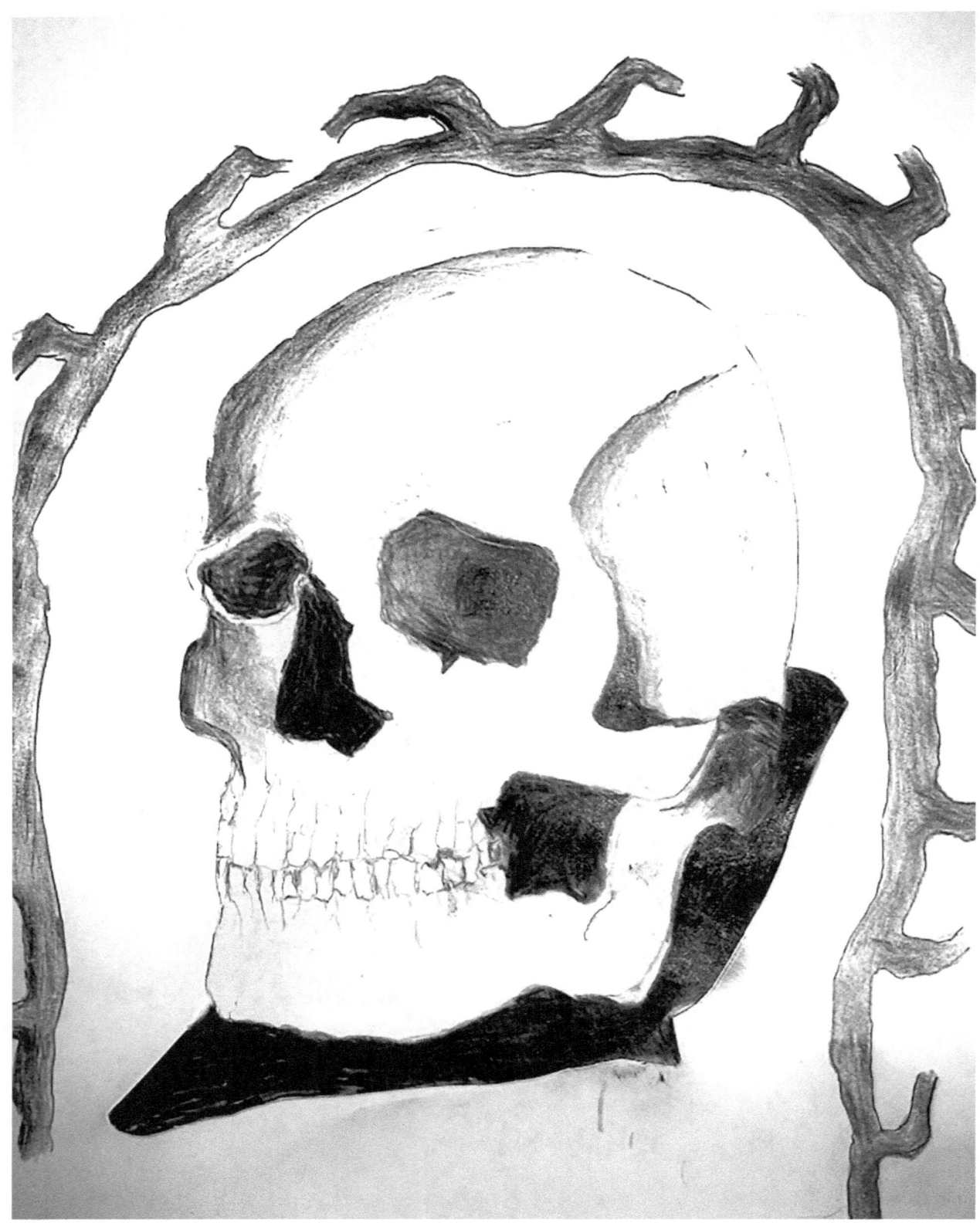

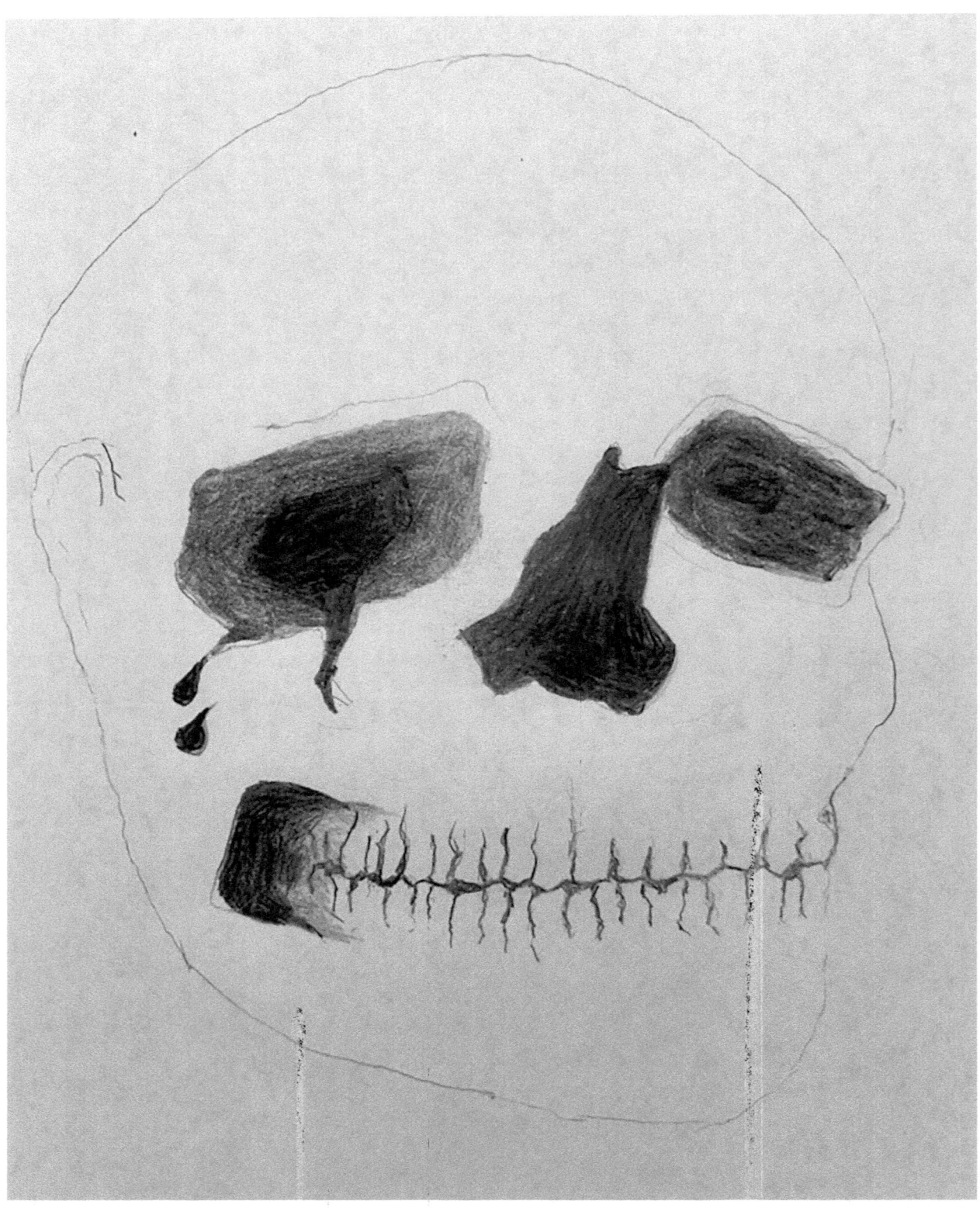

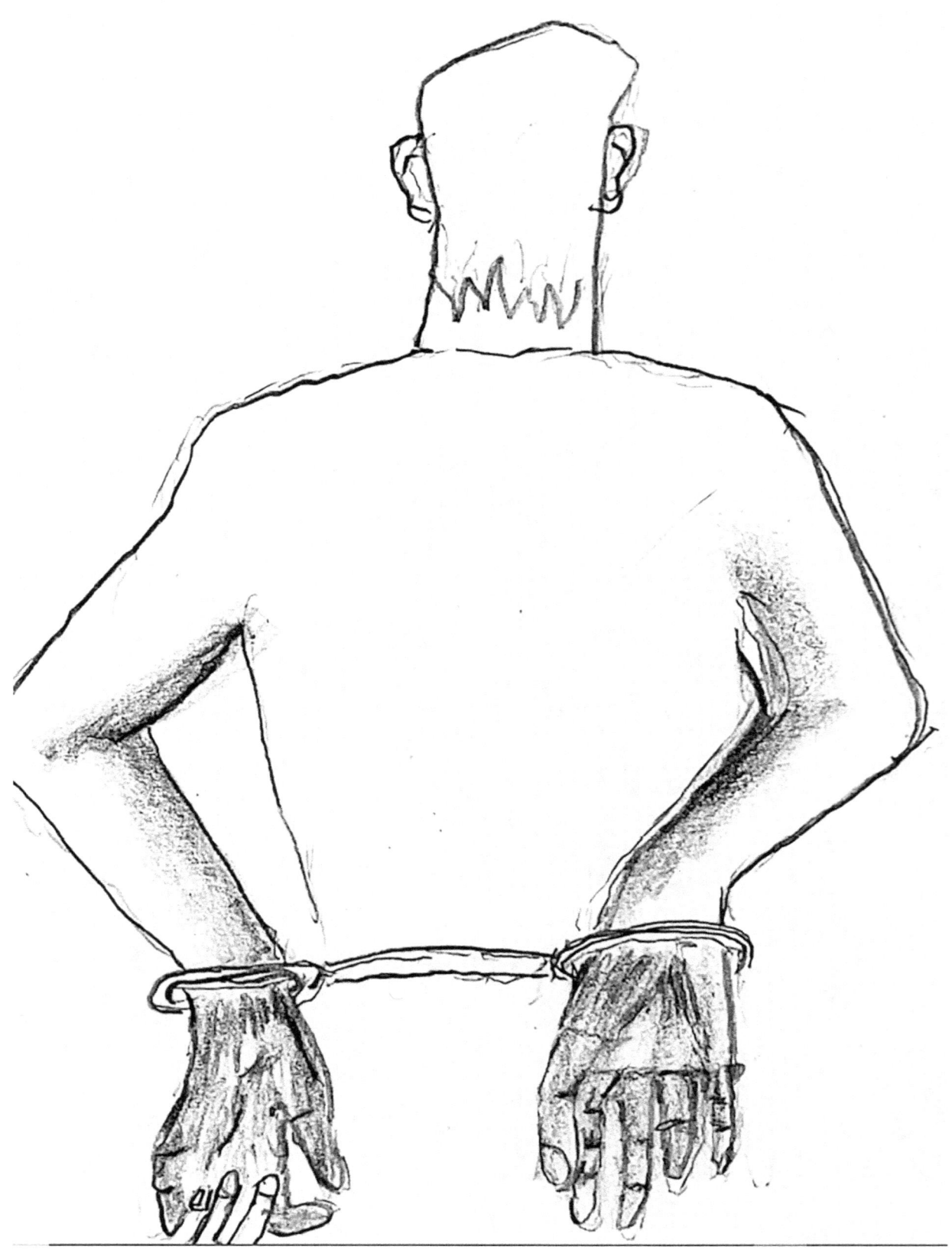

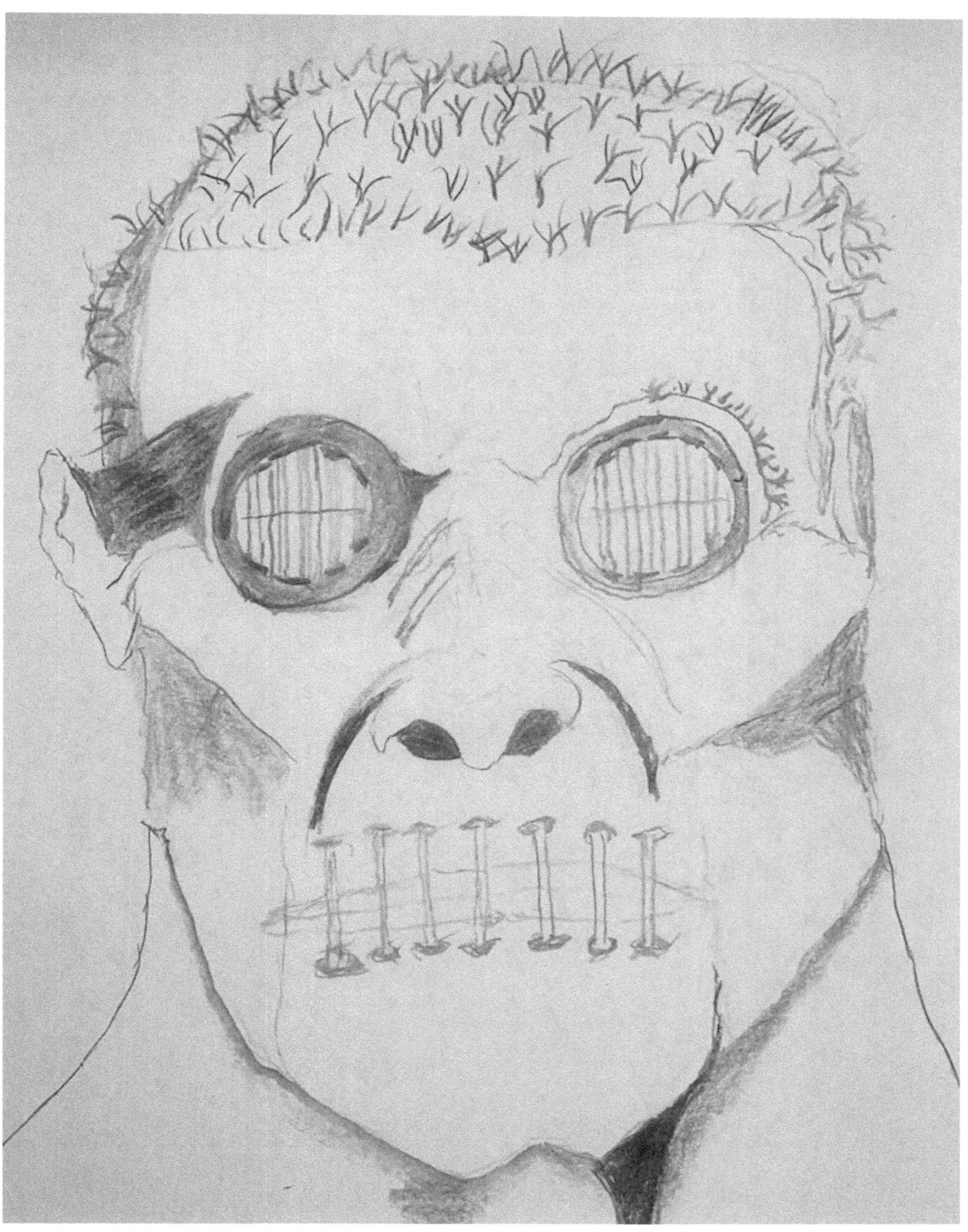

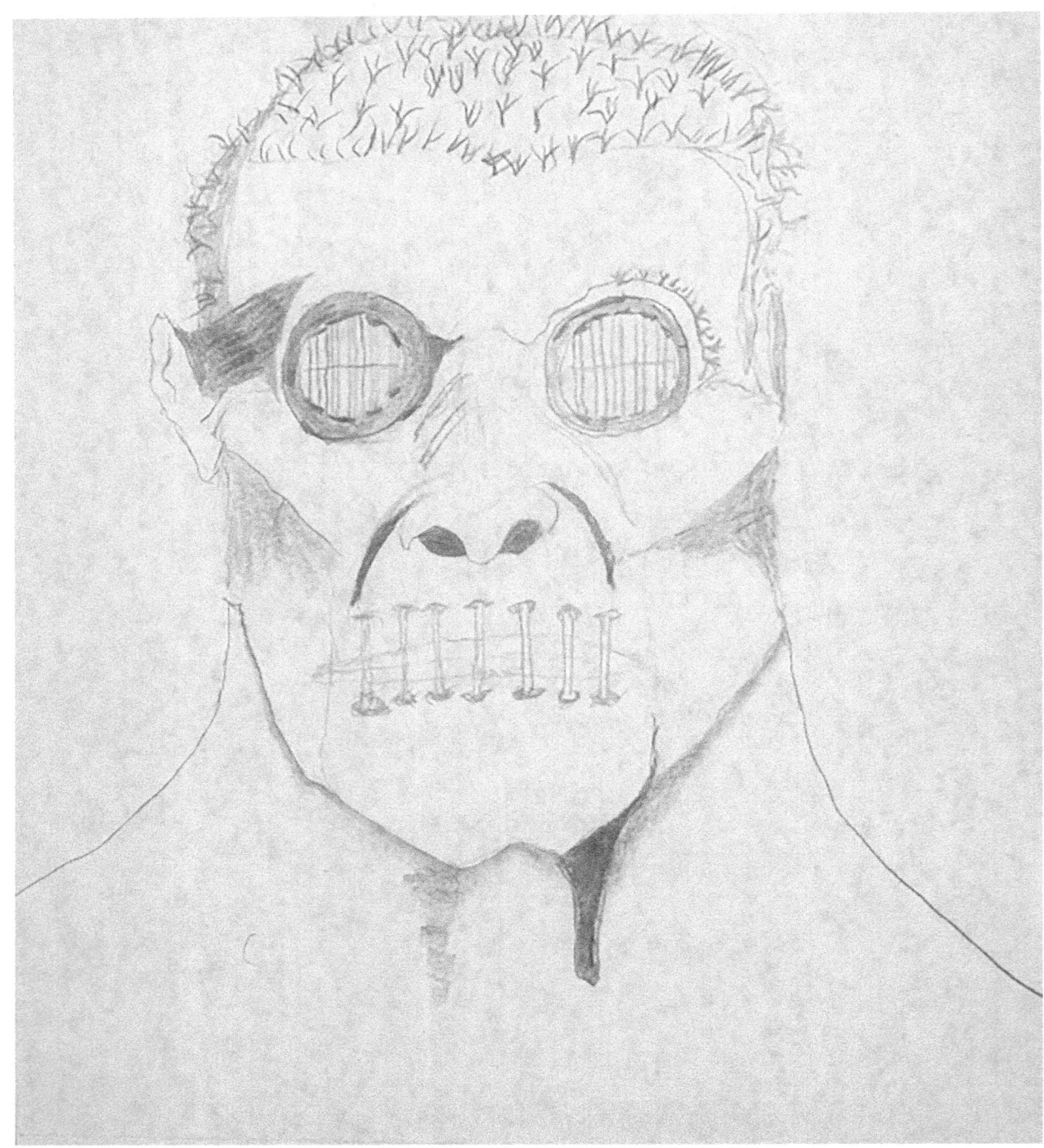

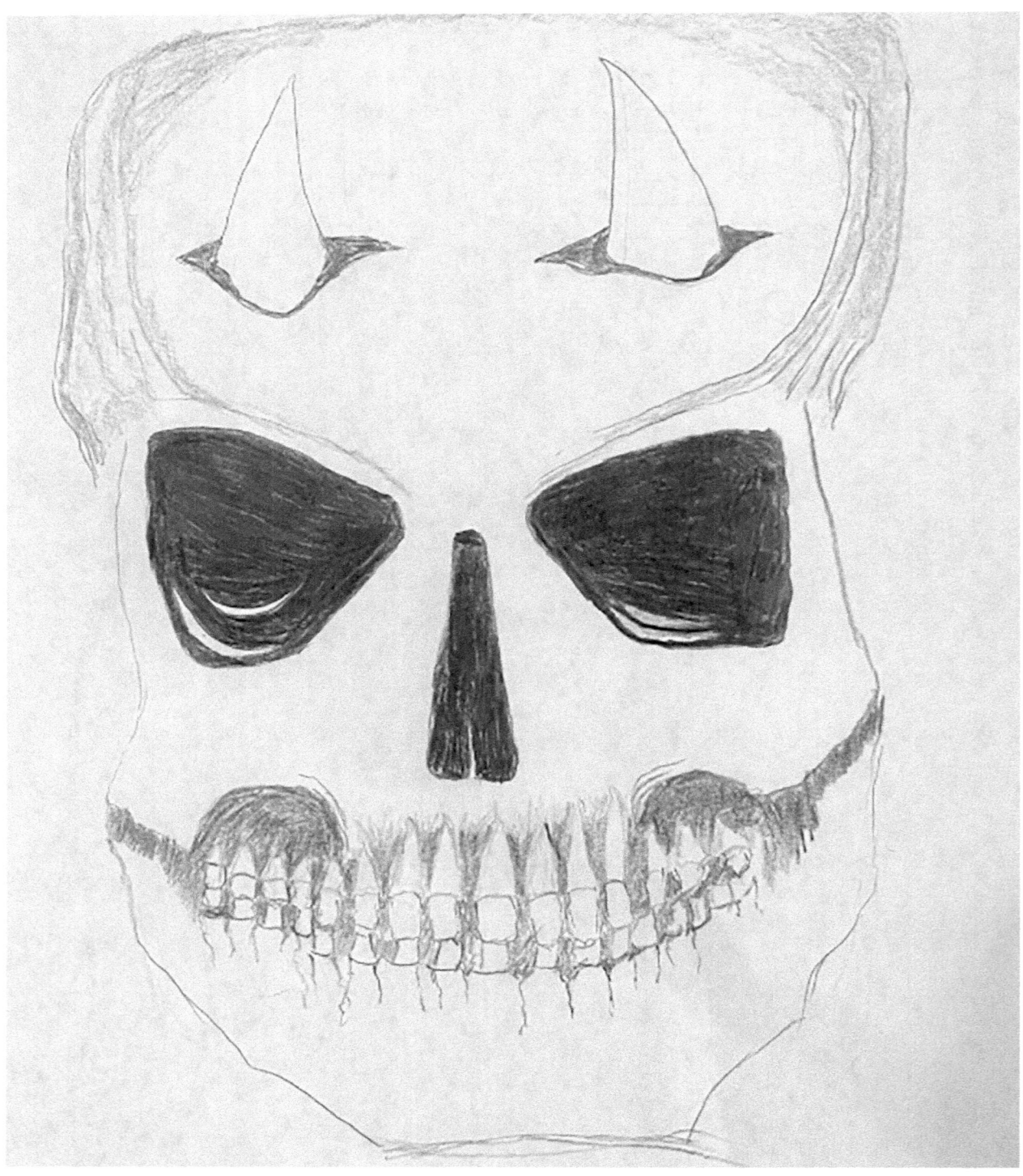

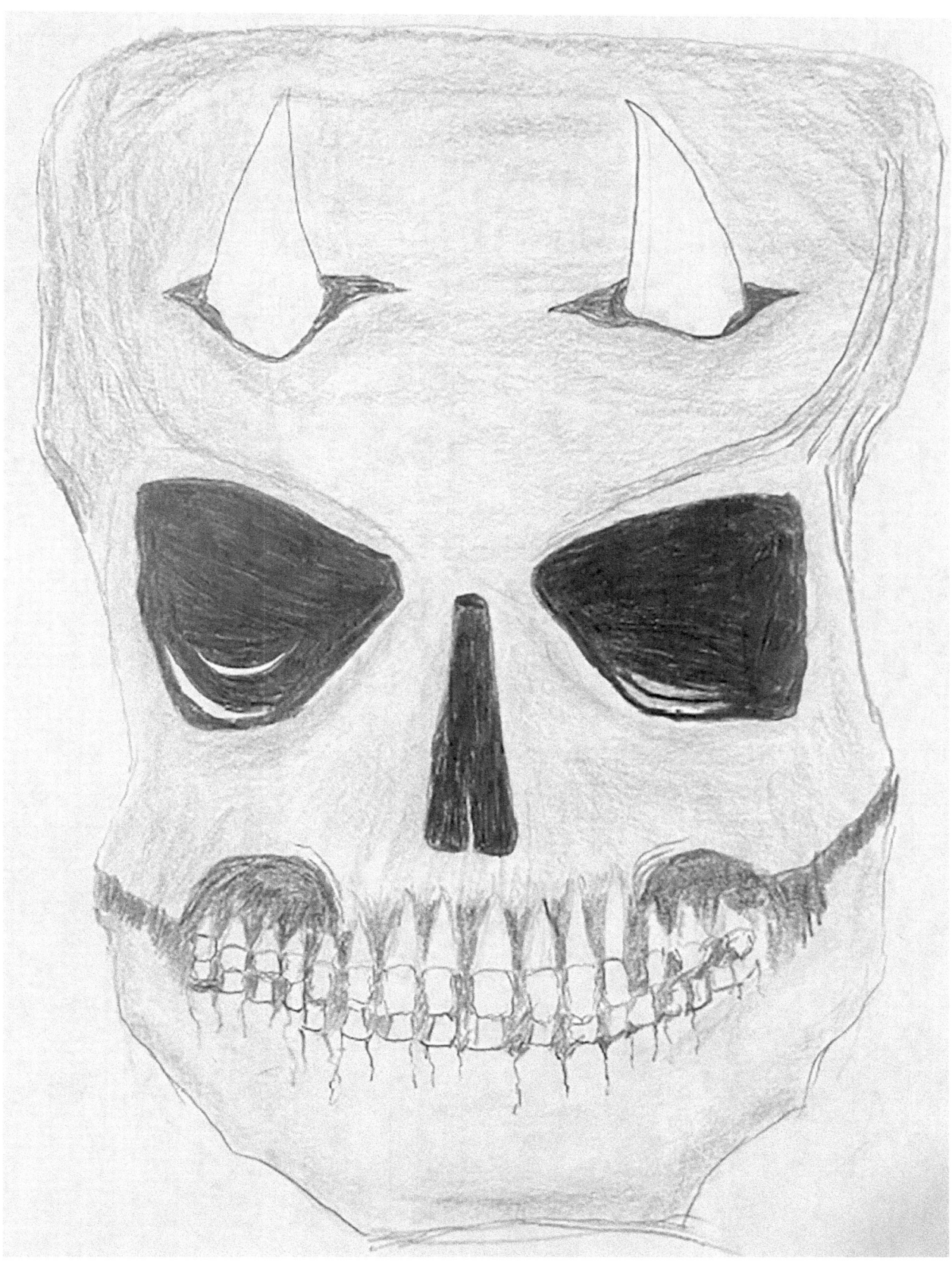

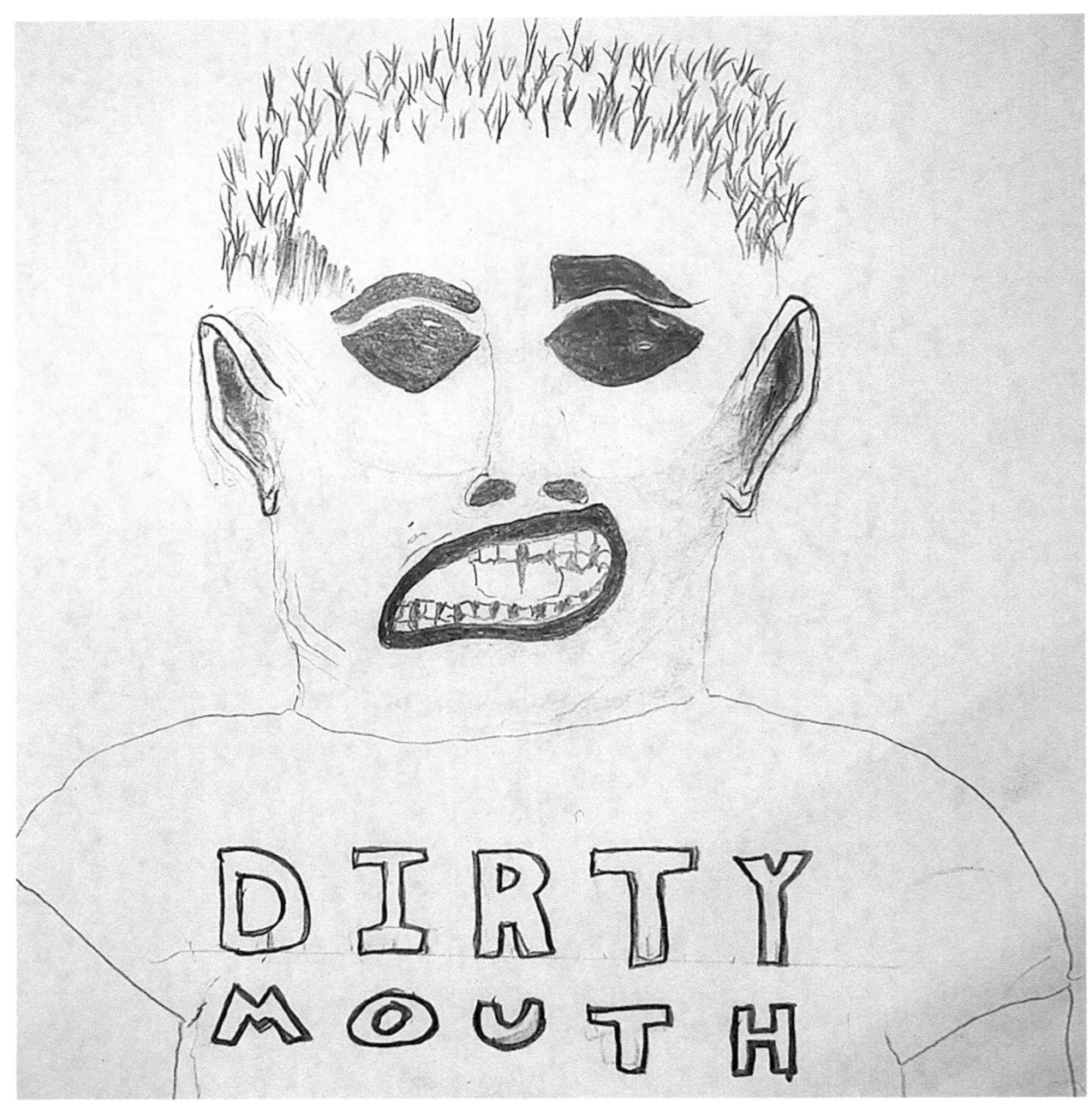

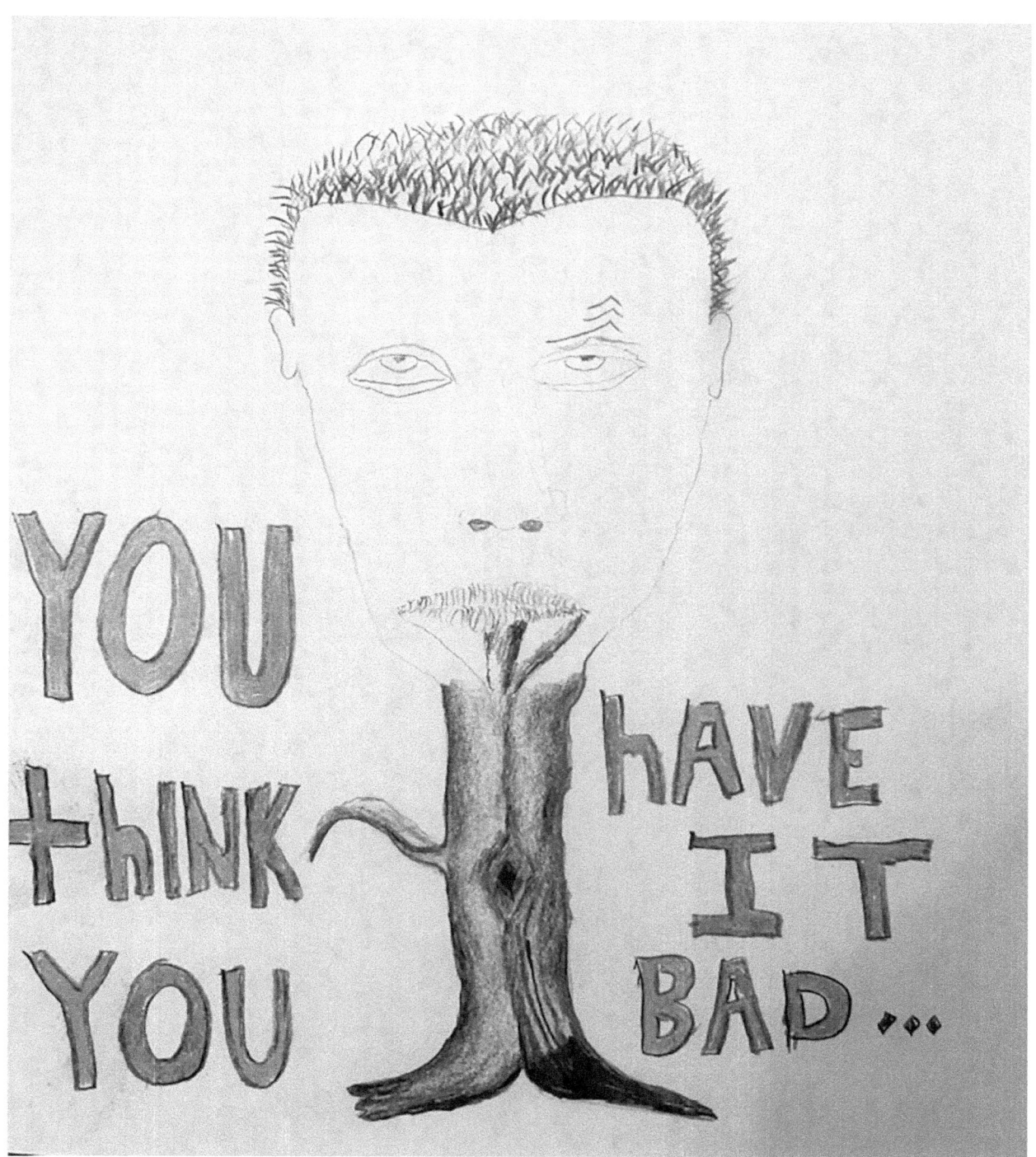

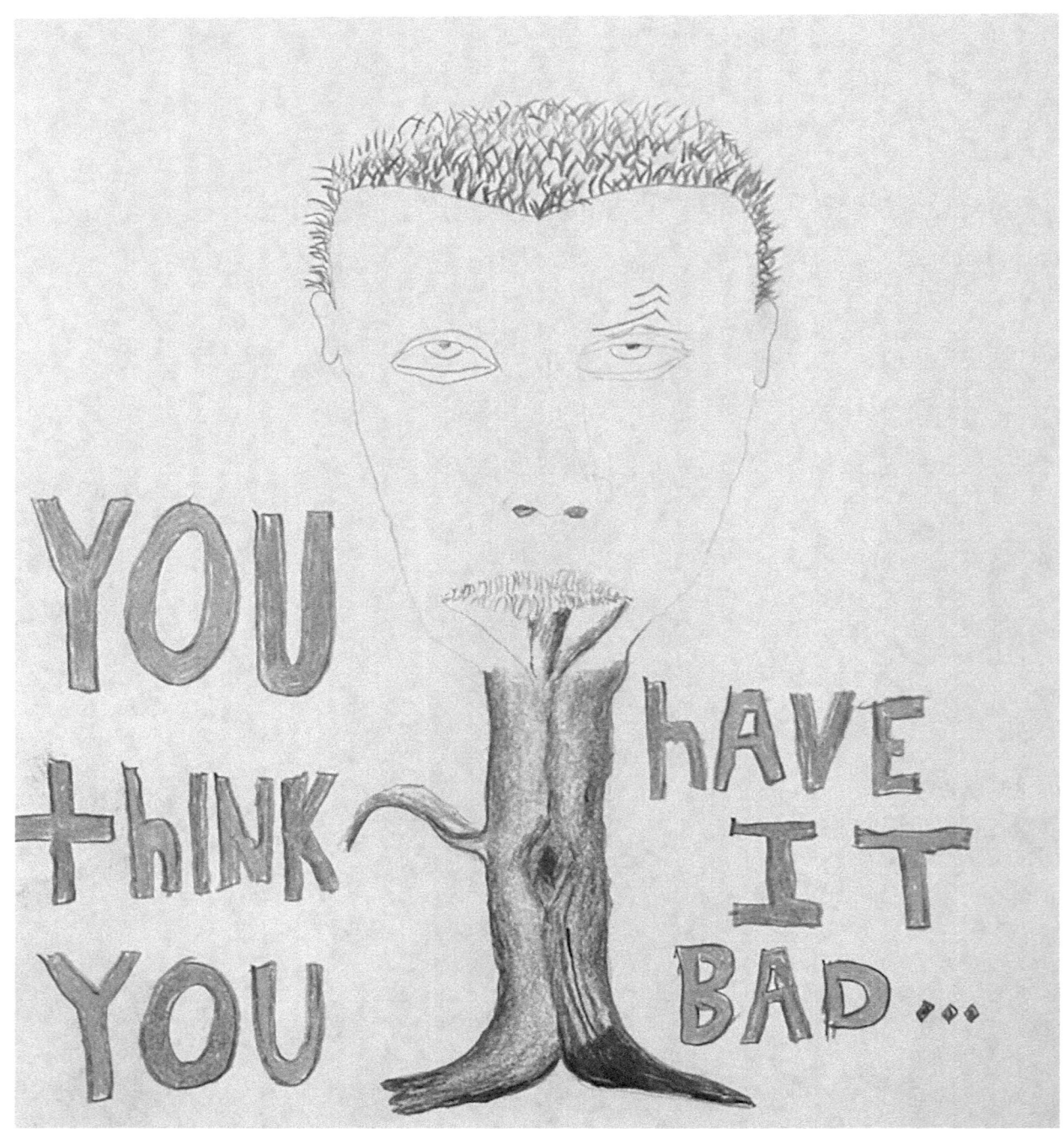

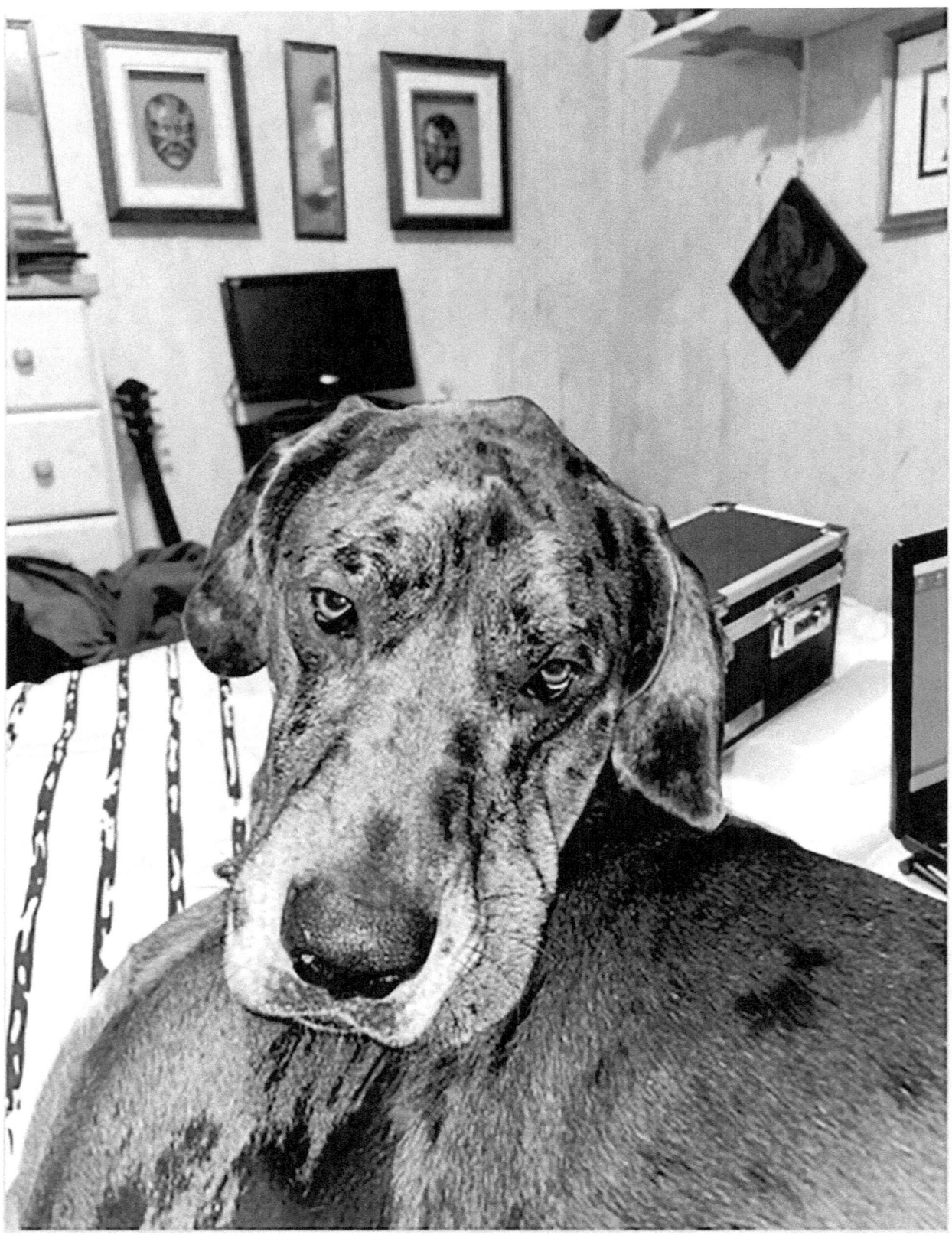

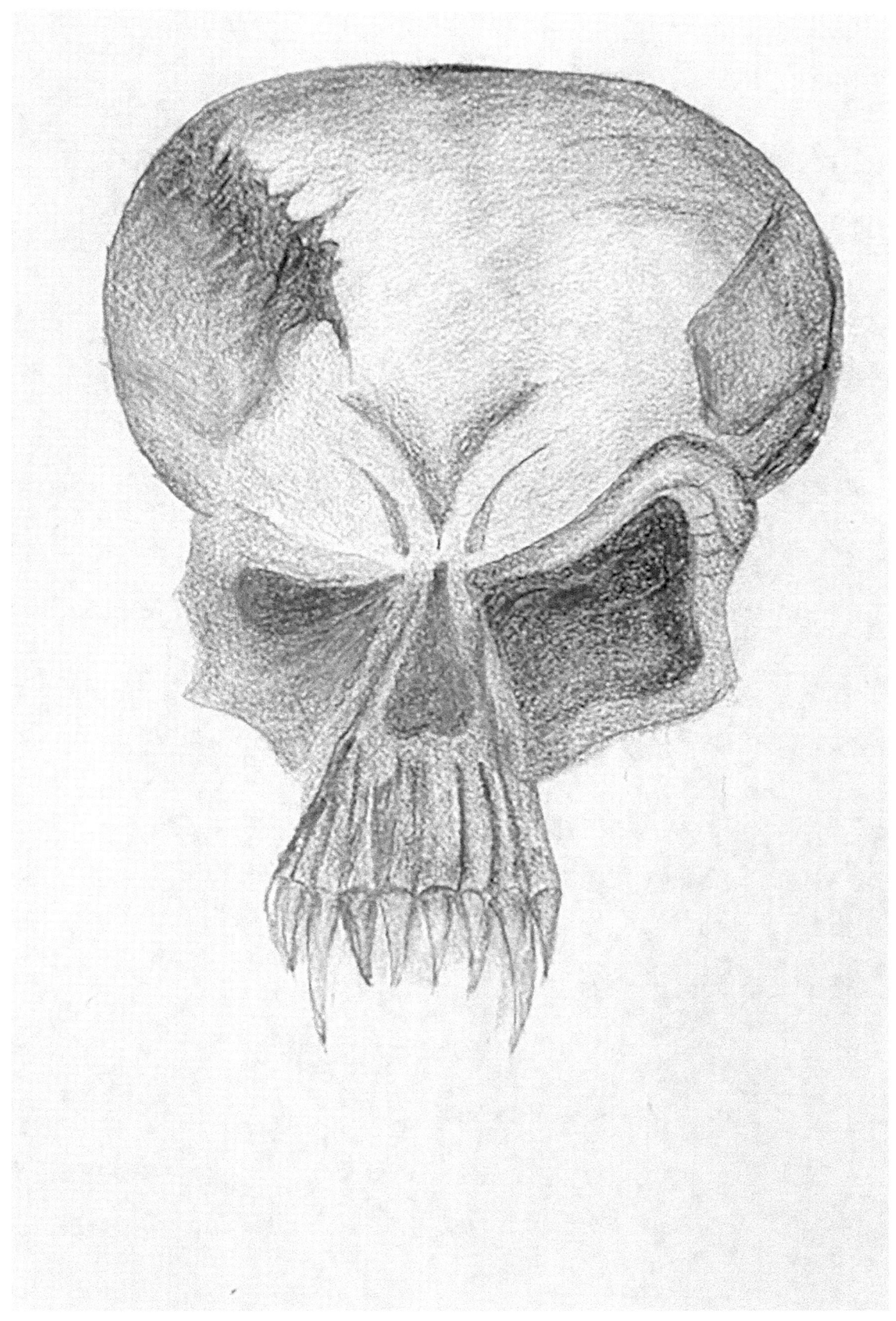

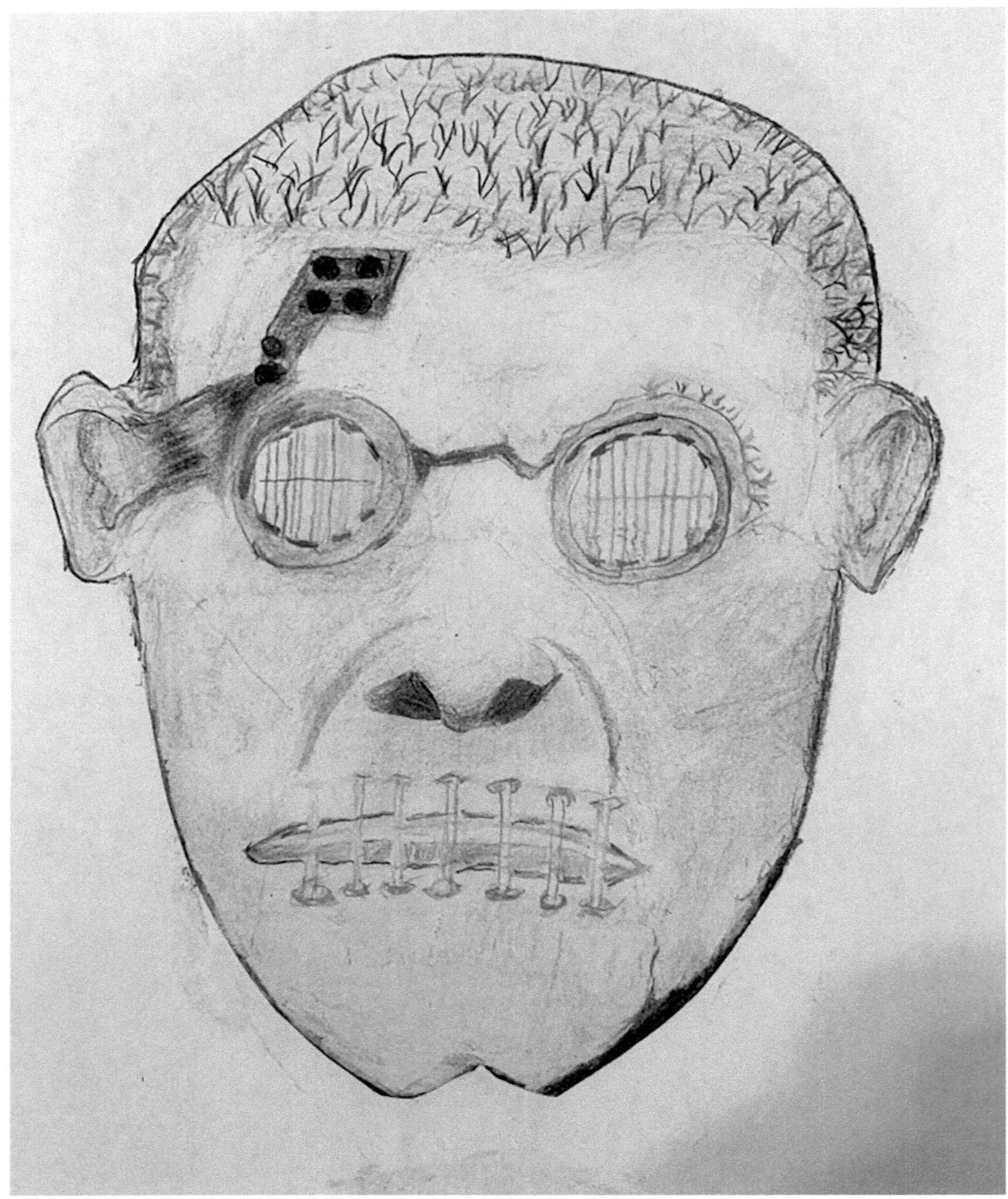

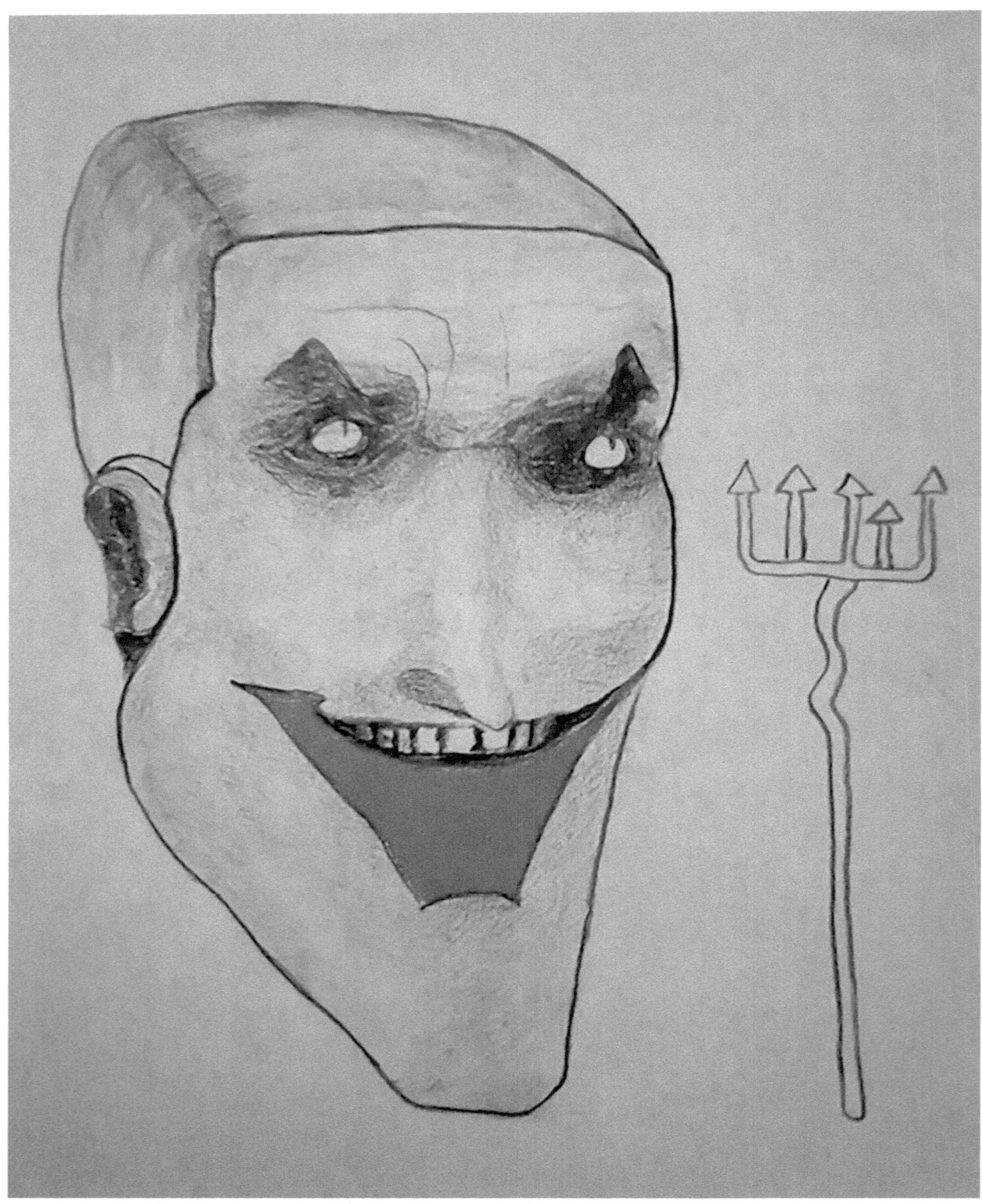

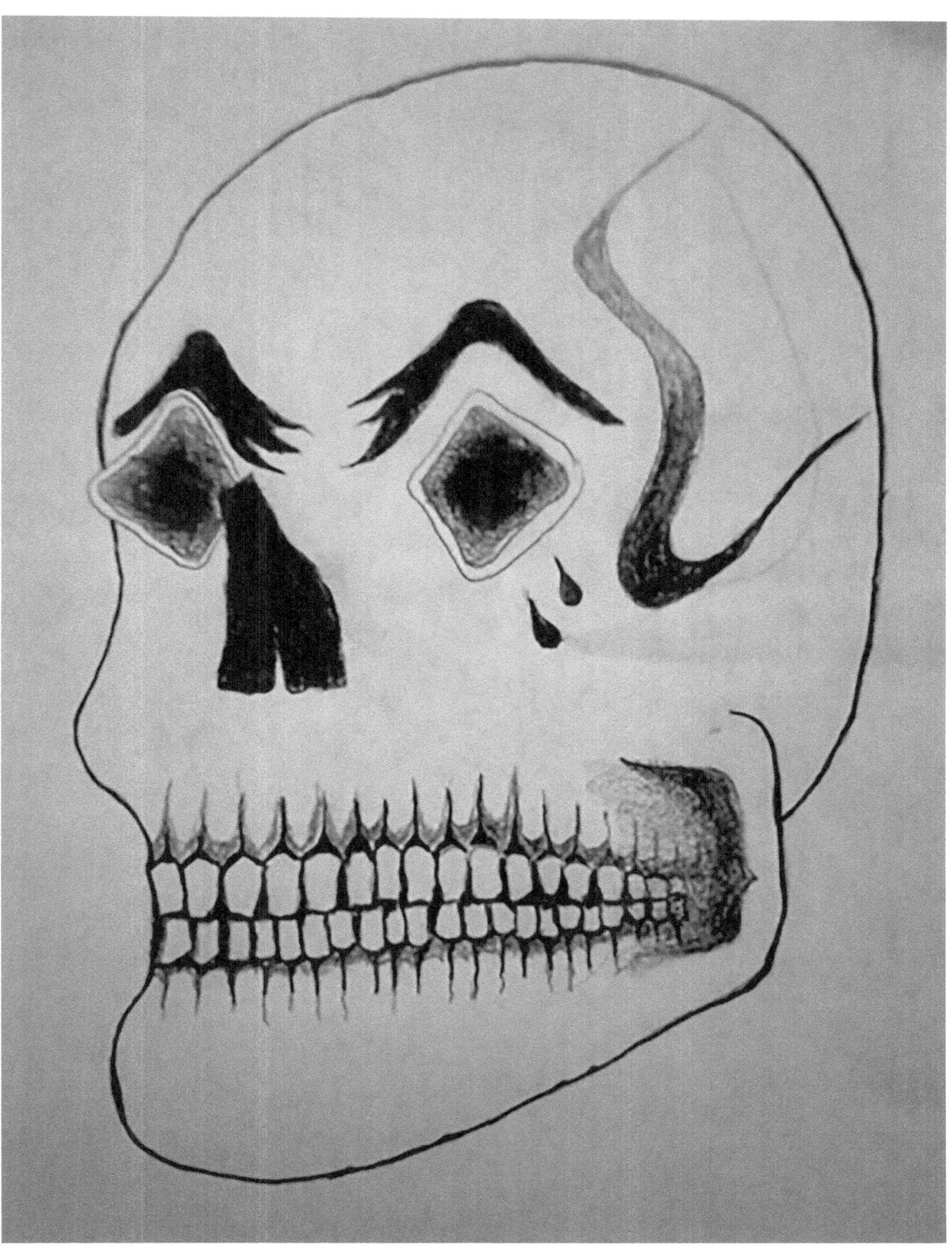

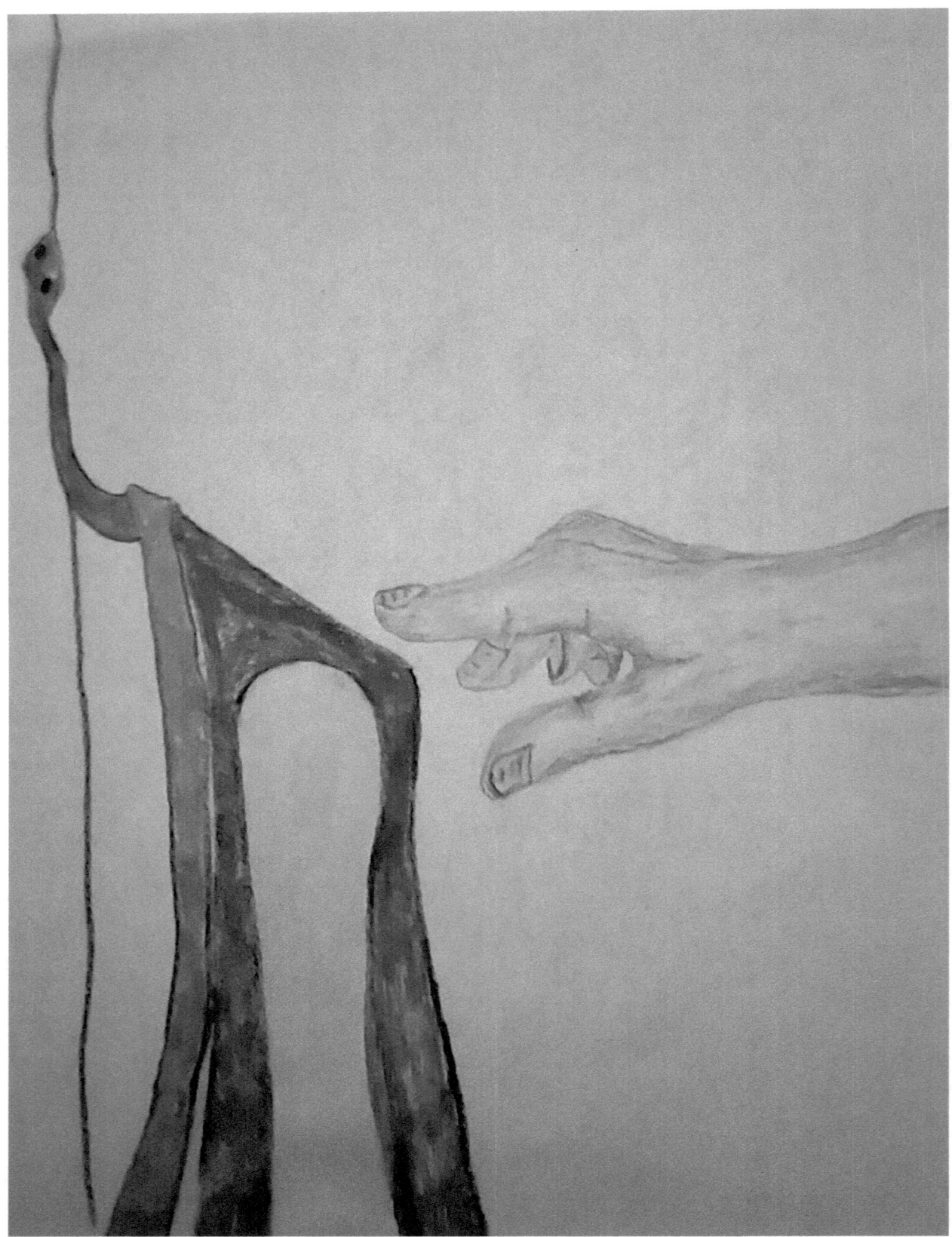

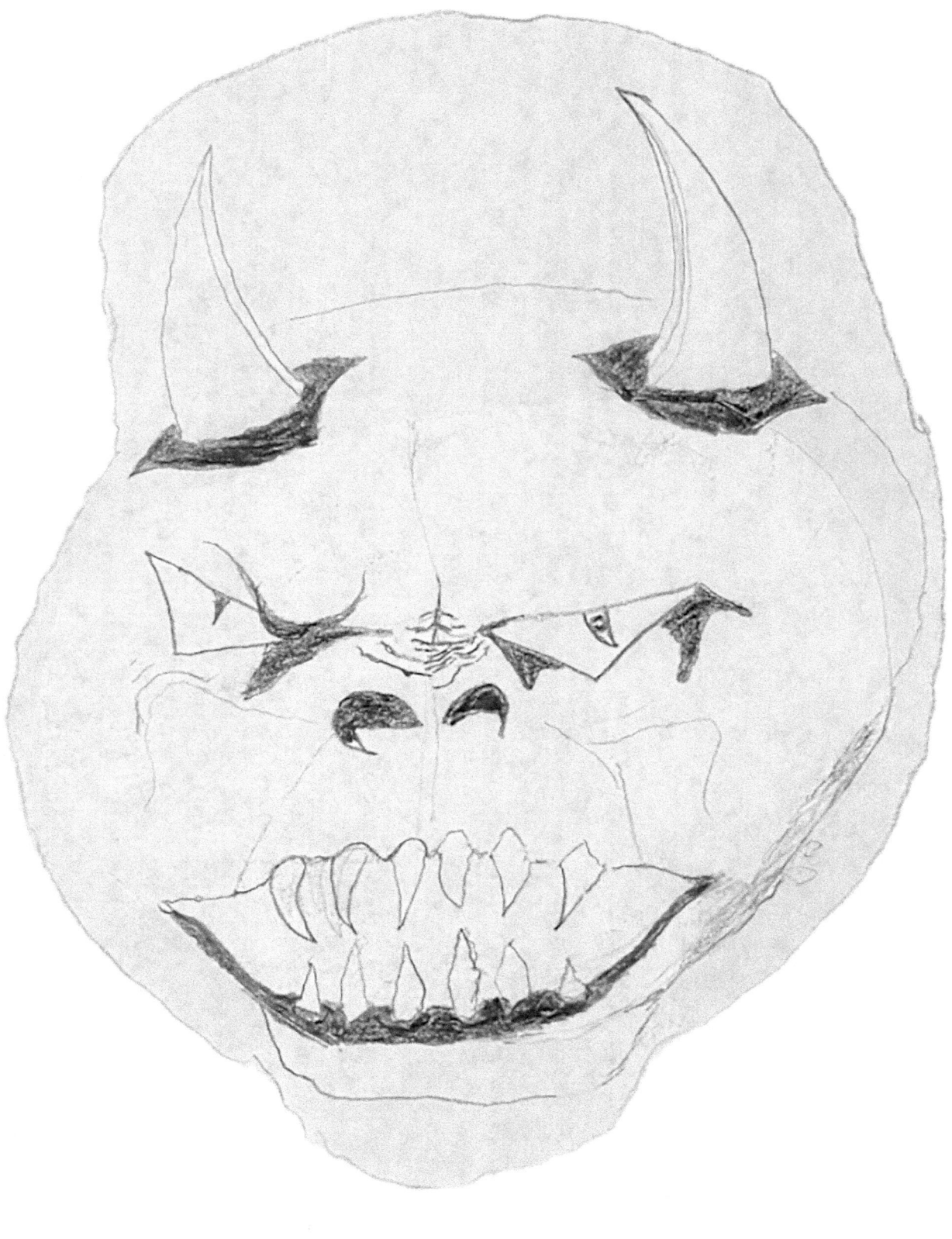